Cheryl,
I love your ☺
Get the HOPES UP!
JS 5-17-14

The

A.P.P.L.E.

Principle

Chris D. Estes

Title: *The A.P.P.L.E. Principle*

By: Chris D. Estes

Publisher: Chris D. Estes

Lexington, KY

The typical result one can expect to achieve is nothing. The "typical" person never gets to the end of this book. The "typical" person fails to implement anything. Thus they earn nothing. Zero. No income. And perhaps a loss of income. That's because "typical" people do nothing and therefore they achieve nothing. Be atypical. Do something. Implement something. If it doesn't work; make a change...and implement that. Try again...try harder. Persist. And reap the rewards.

The A.P.P.L.E. Principle

Praise from Others

"Chris D. Estes has packed the pages of this book with real life examples for you to copy and implement immediately. *The A.P.P.L.E. Principle* is a 'How to' for success, not only in network marketing, but in any area of life or business. The entire principle is so simple and applicable, I wish I had thought of it!"

- John C. Maxwell
New York Times Best-selling Author
and Leadership Expert

"Chris D. Estes is one of the most inspirational and empowering stories in Network Marketing today. His journey to multimillion-dollar earner in record time is clearly articulated in *The A.P.P.L.E. Principle*. A must read!"

- David Moses
Multimillion-Dollar Earner
in the Network Marketing Profession.

"As I was reading *The A.P.P.L.E. Principle*, I was amazed at the simplicity with which the acronym was broken down, and impressed with the depth of knowledge behind it. I highly recommend this book to anyone who desires to have success in Network Marketing. The principles and philosophies taught in the book will not only help you build a huge team; they will help improve every aspect of your life."

- Mike Sims
Multimillion-Dollar Earner
in the Network Marketing Profession.

Table of Contents

Download and print all tools described in this book at
www.TheAPPLEPrinciple.com

A Note From the Author

Paul Orberson is considered by many to be the greatest network marketer of all time. He is one of the fastest in the history of network marketing to make over $1,000,000 per month. Paul went on to earn seven figures for multiple months in a row, while leading thousands of other individuals to financial independence.

I went to visit Paul a couple of months back at his home in Lexington, Kentucky, and brought along a copy of the manuscript of this book. It was nearing completion, and I was eager to get his feedback and input. Paul's advice to me is sprinkled throughout the chapters of *The A.P.P.L.E. Principle*, adding priceless value and insight, just as it did to the past several years of my life.

I am writing this note just a few short days after Paul's passing. It is hard to express in words how grateful I am, not only for his mentorship, but more importantly his friendship. He truly was a servant leader who created a legacy for himself and his family that will live on through the millions of lives he touched. My hope is that I am able to honor his legacy by extending his reach through my words in this book. Rest in peace, my friend, you will be greatly missed... but never forgotten.

Foreword by Paul Orberson

I've experienced incredible personal growth throughout my network marketing journey. Granted, my path was not without struggles and hardships. In fact, I was tempted to quit countless times, especially in the early days. When I was introduced to Chris' story through mutual connections, it reminded me of my own beginnings in the industry.

Chris had an impressive start with his network marketing career, and on just a part-time basis. I learned he wanted me to speak at one of his big team events for the company he was partnered with. Chris felt that with our similar backgrounds as teachers and coaches, along with the challenging decision of how to balance both worlds, I could give his team a boost. Out of courtesy, I called him back.

Chris was extremely persistent. After that first phone conversation, he would stop by my office to ask questions and learn from my experiences. He was so receptive that I agreed to speak at his team event.

It's been a pleasure getting to know Chris. He is positive and uplifting, a true joy to mentor. We became great friends in the process. I love his focus on being a blessing by serving others. This book keeps true to Chris' *keep it simple* philosophy, one he and I spent hours discussing over the years.

I am honored to be associated with Chris. I am so proud of him. It takes courage to win, and Chris is loaded with courage. His life is a great story in the making. I tell him often that young people like him give old people like me hope.

- Paul Orberson

Acknowledgments

To my friend, Paul
I truly believe that my best days are just ahead
because of the seeds that you planted in my life.

Introduction

My Story...

I've been an athlete my entire life. I didn't say a good one, but an athlete nonetheless. I've played college baseball and competed in several triathlons and duathlons. I followed the direction of those who led me in the importance of going to school and getting good grades, so I could get a good job. And that's what I did. By the year 2000 I had earned an undergraduate degree in education, a master's degree in counseling, and a position as a P.E. teacher and coach at a small middle school in central Kentucky. I taught and coached for eight years, thinking that I had arrived and was fulfilling my calling in life.

I knew from a very early age that I had a talent for teaching and coaching. What I didn't realize then, however, was that those eight years spent in the classroom were not the culmination of what my gifts had in store for me... instead they were training for my calling to teach and coach on a bigger playing field than just a baseball field, or a basketball or tennis court. You see, because *I thought* I had arrived, I'd become complacent, even satisfied with where I was in life. If you break down the word satisfaction, 'satis' is a Latin word that means 'enough'; then add 'action' to it and it means 'enough action'. That was me.

My Mind Was Wandering!

I'm not saying my life was bad; I had plenty to be thankful for, but something was missing. When I taught school, my mind was wandering. When I coached the various sports, my mind was wandering. When I was training for triathlons, my mind was wandering.

Has your mind ever wandered?

Here is what I have since learned: if your mind is wandering from the game you're playing in, then the game you're playing in isn't big enough for you.

I Was Broke...

Even though I had a "good job," I was broke. There was always more month at the end of the money for me. Meaning, with a week to go before the next paycheck, there was no money left in my bank account. I knew that in order for things to change I was going to have to change some things.

I wanted more, but I had no real reason to get out of my routine and no real way to make a change. Then, BAM! Fate intervened and provided me with both. I learned that my first child was on the way. It was unplanned, so the words *shocked* and *terrified* are appropriate to describe how I felt in that moment. It was certainly a blessing in disguise, but at the time it seemed like I was being hit from all angles. I had no clue what I was going to do... and then a knock on my door from a friend changed my life forever.

Then Opportunity Knocked...

When opportunity knocks, you can't be in the backyard looking for a four-leaf clover. You have to be prepared and answer the door. A good friend of mine introduced me to a network marketing company. Because I trusted my friend, I looked at the information and was intrigued with what I read. I did have doubts, though; it sounded too good to be true. After all, what company is going to say something negative about what they're offering? McDonald's isn't going to tell you not to order the Big Mac because it could make you fat. But I did my due diligence and turned to third-party resources to validate the industry, the company, and the product. I began to make a list of people that I knew who could benefit from more time, some additional money, and better health. Even though I lived in a town with only two traffic lights, there were a lot of names on my list.

I Got Started!

The key to getting ahead is getting started, so I got started. I've learned through personal experience that what Zig Ziglar said is true: "You don't have to be great to start, but you have to start to be great."[1] I faced many obstacles in the beginning of my network marketing business. People closest to me ridiculed and opposed what I was doing. I ran around like a chicken with my head cut off, traveling all over the state sharing the business opportunity, with little to show for it. I began to doubt my decision to do the business. I was unorganized, and my doubt paralyzed me from always taking action. But I'm competitive, so I stayed the course. After several months of sowing the seed I began to finally see some signs of fruit.

My Reality Changed...

As my business grew, so did my need for organization. I turned to mentors for guidance, people who had achieved the kind of success I was hoping to achieve. I began to weave some of their suggestions in with my personal philosophy. Through trial and error, I've created a principle that is so simple to do, I could teach my former middle school students to master it. The principle didn't make a huge impact in a day... but daily, over time, it has changed my life forever. It all started with focusing on five daily actions that, done consistently, led me to where I am today.

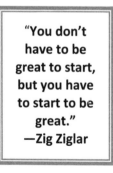

"You don't have to be great to start, but you have to start to be great."
—Zig Ziglar

The A.P.P.L.E. Principle

We have all heard the saying, "An apple a day keeps the doctor away." Well, what if it's true? What if you could do something as simple as eating one apple each day and, bite by bite, control your total health and well-being! Now consider this: what if the apple wasn't an apple at all, but instead an intentional set of daily actions that build over time, bite by bite, the life you've always wanted. Well, I have some great news for us all.

IT IS TRUE!

The A.P.P.L.E. Principle is a simple daily system that, when followed consistently, can lead anyone from where they currently are to where they desire to be, in any aspect of life. Please allow me to take you, one bite at a time, through the system I used in my own life to get from a place of complacency to a life unlimited.

1

"A" stands for ATTITUDE

"The greatest discovery of all time is that a person can change his future by merely changing his attitude."
- Oprah Winfrey

You can Study for the Test, but not the Pop Quiz.

Life has funny timing. As I was writing this chapter on ATTITUDE, I was being challenged to live out what I was teaching, to walk the walk, as they say. My network marketing business was flourishing, and I had reached a rank in my company that paid out a substantial bonus. This type of success can't be achieved alone; it's a compilation of the efforts of many. To properly recognize the efforts of my team and show my gratitude, I had decided to use the bonus money to fund a dream vacation. This memory-making recognition retreat would be with the top leaders that I had the privilege of building the business with. Several months of planning and preparation were poured into this trip to make sure that every detail was just right. The limo bus picked the party of sixteen up at my home. After we arrived at the airport, we checked our luggage all the way to destination, and took off right on time. I was breathing easy; I so badly wanted this to be a perfect trip, and all was going just as planned... then, POP QUIZ!

I remember checking my watch at just the moment we were scheduled to be landing in one of the most beautiful places on the face of the planet: Bora Bora's St. Regis Resort and Spa in Tahiti. But instead, because of bad weather and missed flights, I was sitting in an airport wearing the same clothes that I'd been wearing for 48 hours. To make matters worse, no one could tell us when the next flight to Tahiti was going to depart; thousands of dollars, and more importantly our time, were being lost.

For many, this would have been a devastating turn of events, one that would have caused major whining and headache. But, as I looked around at the company I was with, I noticed there were no frowns on their faces and no complaints from their lips. These people and their spouses were still happy, excited, and genuinely enjoying themselves. Why was that, do you think? I'll tell you why... each of these winners had taken the first bite out of their A.P.P.L.E. They knew that every morning you get up and you have a choice:

- You can choose to get better or be bitter.
- You can see your cup half filled or half spilled.
- You can choose to have a winning ATTITUDE or a whining ATTITUDE.

As John Maxwell says, "Your ATTITUDE doesn't make *the* difference, but your ATTITUDE *is* the difference maker"[1]

There Is No Such Thing As Luck!

It's amazing to me how one simple word can control everything else in your life. How blessed you are, how loved you feel, how successful you become, and even how "lucky" you are perceived to be, is all determined by the ATTITUDE that you have. Your life, or how the world treats you, is nothing more than a reflection of your own ATTITUDE. According to Jim Rohn, "Our ATTITUDE toward life determines life's ATTITUDE toward us." Your ATTITUDE is not something you were born with; it's not formed by your genetic makeup. Instead, your ATTITUDE is a learned behavior. It's shaped and molded continually by your environment, by who you hang around with, and whose philosophy you buy into. Think about the power that you could have if you could just choose to have a winning ATTITUDE.

IT'S A CHOICE...

Take Bite #1

The first bite of the A.P.P.L.E. that I eat everyday stands for the word ATTITUDE. I will tell you that simply knowing that your ATTITUDE is your choice does not make choosing to have a winning ATTITUDE a breeze. It's not easy to always think positively or have enthusiasm when nothing seems to be working in your favor. It's not easy to keep a smile on your face when there is a mortgage staring you down or when multiple credit card payments are due. It's not easy to keep your hopes up when you've worked all day at your full-time job only to then move to your second and third jobs just to make ends meet. It's not easy when the people you thought would partner with you in business say, "NO."

Do it Anyway.

It's not easy, but it's doable. And it's doable because it is your choice. You have a choice; you can either get better or be bitter. That was my life back in 2008; I was living on instant gratification and pushing off all things that weren't easy until later in hopes that things would just work themselves out. But according to Joel Osteen, "Our lives don't get better by chance, our lives get better by change."[2] So on those days when you just don't feel like

> Keep in mind that the very first bite is always the hardest one to swallow.

eating your A.P.P.L.E. (and believe me, you will have more than your share of those days), please keep in mind that the very first bite is always the hardest one to swallow. It's time to stop doing what you've been doing and start fresh right now by taking the first bite out of your A.P.P.L.E.! It's time to choose to have a winning ATTITUDE!

CHOOSE NOW!

No Matter the Circumstance...

I heard a story once about two men who were patients in the same hospital room. Every day the man closest to the window shared with his friend what he saw outside, describing it in great detail, so his roommate could enjoy the view even though he was confined to his bed. "Today, I see a beautiful sunrise," he'd say. "The kids are out there playing. The trees are blossoming," and on and on. Each day the bedridden patient looked forward to hearing his roommate's report on the outside world. It was the highlight of his day.

> "Circumstances are the rulers of the weak; they are but the instruments of the wise."
> — Samuel Lover

One day, the patient next to the window became so excited. "Oh, you should see it! There's a parade coming by with a marching band, kids and adults celebrating something and having such a good time." After several weeks, the patient next to the window passed away, so his friend asked the nurse if he could have the bed next to the window, so he could see all the great scenes of activity outside. "Why, certainly," the nurse replied as she moved the patient to the bed next to the window. But when the man looked out the window, much to his surprise, all he could see was a brick wall. The patient called the nurse back and said, "Hey, wait a minute! My friend that passed away described all the beautiful scenes for several weeks, and I can't see anything but a wall!" The nurse smiled and said, "Sir, didn't you realize that your friend was blind? He chose to see a beautiful life from the inside out."

Samuel Lover said, "Circumstances are the rulers of the weak; they are but the instruments of the wise."[3] No matter what circumstances you may be facing, you can choose to see a beautiful life, you can choose to have a winning ATTITUDE, and you can start that now!

YOU HAVE EVERYTHING YOU NEED!

If Only...

It's an epidemic in this country, widespread and growing rapidly. I like to call it the "If Only" disease! It can be easily diagnosed by simply listening for these phrases:

> If only I had more time, I would...
> If only I had more money, I would...
> If only I had more experience, I would...
> If only I were gifted in that area, I would...

I run into people all the time who have the "If Only's"! They want more than they have and dream about a brighter future, but they don't believe that they can get to where they want to go from where they currently are. My message to them is simple: you already have everything you need!

Back in 2008, when I first enrolled in network marketing, I was going against the grain, to say the least. I was the first one in my town to get started with the company, actually the first one in the state of Kentucky. I

> I run into people all the time who have the "If Only's"

had caught a vision of what the additional income could mean for my family and myself. Excited is not a big enough word to describe the emotion that I had placed on this opportunity. You can imagine the shock I felt at the ridicule and objections that I faced right out of the gate, and from some of my closest friends and family members at that. "You're a teacher and coach! You don't know anything about business and you don't have any money to get started!" Or, "Are you talking about network marketing? You can't do that, it's a scam!" I began to question myself, thinking maybe it's true... maybe I don't have any business doing this... maybe I should just keep doing what I've been doing.

You may be reading this right now and are trying to make a change, and in doing so you are catching some flack from those who are closest to you. You may even be where I was, doubting your decision to go against the grain and strive for something more than an average life. You're starting to show symptoms of the "If Only" disease. Well, back in 2008 I caught a slight case of the "If Only's"! *If only* I had business experience, maybe I could do this... *If only* I had more money, maybe I could get started... *If only* I had more free time, maybe I could find some people... *If only* it were June not July, maybe I could make this work. Friend, let me tell you something that my friend and mentor, Paul Orberson told me: "If frogs had pockets, they'd carry guns and shoot snakes. But frogs don't have pockets, and frogs don't shoot snakes."

Someone Else's B.S.

I want to encourage you to never let someone else's B.S. hinder you. Get your mind out of the gutter; what I mean by B.S. is Belief System! Some people, *in some cases even you*, don't have enough belief in themselves to try anything new, so they spread their doubt on you. Remember, there are only two types of people who will tell you that you can't be successful with what you're doing: those who are afraid to try, and those who are afraid you will succeed. So, be cautious of whose B.S. you buy into, knowing that if you buy other

> If you buy into other people's opinions, you'd better be prepared to buy into their lifestyle.

people's opinions, you'd better be prepared to buy into their lifestyle.

Trust Your Gifts.

I thought long and hard about my decision to get started, and even continued to question my decision after I took the initial plunge into the business. But the great story of David and Goliath put everything in perspective for me. You see, when the Israelite army looked up at the Philistine giant, they said, "He's so big, we can't kill him!" But the little shepherd boy, David, looked at the same giant, and said, "He's so big, I can't miss!"

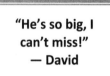

"He's so big, I can't miss!"
— David

It's all a matter of perspective and ATTITUDE. So, it turned out that all of the attributes that I possessed as a schoolteacher, coach, and competitive athlete were exactly the skills that I needed to make it work for me. Plus, all of the "If Only's" that I thought would cause me not to succeed were actually the reasons that caused me to *win*. I didn't have business experience, but I had people skills. I didn't have money, but I had a card called "Master," and a burning desire for more. I didn't have time, because I was teaching and coaching, but because of my schedule I was around a lot of other busy people who were eager to have better health, more money, and time freedom as well! Remember, the key to getting ahead in life is to get started.

Your Flavor Creates Your Favor.

I already had everything that I needed to make my dreams a reality and you already have everything you need. This approach is so much better than thinking, "If I just had more money, if my loan had gone through, if they had been my friend, if I had a better personality..." WRONG! If you needed any of those things to fulfill your calling or have an abundant

15

life, God would have given it to you! This is not to say that we shouldn't develop our talents and skills.

Even top athletes still need to practice and get better. But the seeds of greatness are already there. You may not have as much as someone else, but that's ok — you're not competing against them, you're only competing with yourself. Your only challenge is to be the best you that you can be! You're the worst anyone else, but you're the best you in existence. So don't go out trying to be someone else. Remember, it's your flavor that creates your favor.

I took advantage of the opportunity I was presented with at my garage door during the summer of 2008. I shook off every doubt that had been laid on me because I knew that if I wanted it bad enough, I would find a way, and if not... I would cling to one of those excuses. Remember, when you buy your own excuses, you will soon try to sell them to someone else. So, I went to work competing only against myself, each day setting a goal to do a little more and be a little more than I was the day before. I chose daily to have a winning ATTITUDE and to not give up on my hopes and dreams. Success didn't appear overnight, but instead it came slowly with each right choice I made... day by day, inch by inch, and bite by bite.

Stop Waiting and Start Being.

> **A time comes when you need to stop waiting for the person you want to become, and start being the person you want to be.**

A time comes when you need to stop waiting for the person you want to become, and start being the person you want to be. A time comes when you have to take responsibility for the choices and actions of your past that brought you to where you currently are. A time comes when you have to take responsibility for the choices and actions you will make today that will lead you to where you want to be in

16

the future. There is nothing holding you back except you and your doubts about you. It's easy to stay the same; it's easy not to change. Be aware though, that life will give you whatever you will accept. If you will accept average and ordinary, life will give you average and ordinary. If you will accept having relationship problems, life will give you relationship problems. If you will accept having financial issues, life will give you financial issues.

Bring on the "Haters!"

In the summer of 2010 I made a decision to leave my teaching and coaching position and pursue my network marketing business full time. My business was growing steadily, and I felt good about the direction the team and I were moving in. Then one day I saw a post that someone had put on Facebook about me:

"Chris has never been in network marketing before. He's not qualified to lead in this company or in this industry. He needs to go back to his day job."

At first this bothered me. My focus had always been on helping others and serving the team. Why would anyone feel the need to plant a seed of doubt at this point? I have since realized that the only taste of success that some people get is when they take a bite out of yours. You see, "Haters" only get loud when you do things that matter! Jon Acuff, in his book *Start,* said, "If you want to be average, if you want to be vanilla right to the grave, hate will give you a free pass."[4] But when you understand that with success come the "Haters," you can only hope for increasing numbers.

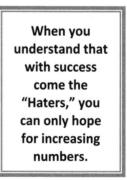

When you understand that with success come the "Haters," you can only hope for increasing numbers.

People may not approve of you or what you are trying to do, but don't worry about it. Other people don't determine your future, and other people can't stop the plan you have for your life. My advice would be to stop thinking so much on all of the things you don't have and stop worrying so much about other people's opinions of you. After all, Steve Maraboli said, "If you fuel your journey on the opinions of others, you WILL run out of gas."[5]

All They Had Was Enough...

- David was the smallest male in his family, and all he had was a slingshot and five stones, and that worked out okay for him.

- Moses had a speech impediment and only an ordinary old stick, but that worked out okay for him, too.

- Samson was only one man with the jawbone of a donkey, but that was all he needed to defeat an entire army.

Don't let the thoughts of what you don't have make you underestimate the power of what you do have. It may look small and it may look insignificant, like all the odds are against you.... but get your hopes up; you have everything you need right now to get you to where you want to go.

It's easy to say, "If I had _____, I would..." It's easy to make excuses when you hold onto a "lacking mindset," feeling like you don't have enough. But you do have enough. Write yourself a prescription for the "If Only" disease: *five bites out of your A.P.P.L.E. everyday, with the first one being a winning ATTITUDE.*

R_X

*5 bites out of your A.P.P.L.E. everyday,
with the first one being a winning ATTITUDE :*

IT'S NOT ALWAYS SUNSHINE AND RAINBOWS!

I'm a huge fan of the Rocky movies. In 2006, when *Rocky 5* came out, I watched it so many times I could recite most of the movie by memory. My favorite scene was when Rocky was talking to his son about how to succeed in life.

"Let me tell you something you already know. The world ain't all sunshine and rainbows. It's a very mean and nasty place, and I don't care how tough you are, it will beat you to your knees and keep you there permanently if you let it. You, me, or nobody is gonna hit as hard as life. But it ain't about how hard you hit. It's about how hard you can get hit and keep moving forward; how much you can take and keep moving forward. That's how winning is done! Now, if you know what you're worth, then go out and get what you're worth. But you gotta be willing to take the hits, and not pointing fingers saying you ain't where you wanna be because of him, or her, or anybody. Cowards do that, and that ain't you. You're better than that!"[6]

19

We've all faced setbacks and disappointments. We've all experienced a loss and then taken some time to wallow in our self-pity. The result of actually becoming a success or a failure, however, is determined by how long you choose to stay there. If you are prone to having an ATTITUDE of self-pity, you are whipped before you start. I encourage you to be prepared for the storms so that when it starts to rain you don't let discouragement steal your passion and your future. Losing your will to fight for your hopes and dreams is a death sentence for you.

When people come to me and ask for advice on how to handle the bad days, I simply remind them that the situation they are currently in is not meant to be permanent. In fact,

We must all choose to make failures our steppingstones, not our tombstones.

"The Lord has plans to prosper and not harm you, to give you hope and a future" (Jeremiah 29:11, NIV). Those bad days are not meant to be permanent; however, they can become permanent if you choose to stop fighting for your future. We must all choose to make failures our steppingstones, not our tombstones.

There have been plenty of times in my life when doubt, fear, and discouragement tried to talk me into giving in and giving up. Sure, when facing critics, doubters, and skeptics, it would be easier to just give up and join them on their path to mediocrity and complacency, but I want to encourage you to set your sights past the hardships of the day and create your own path. Don't give up and give in; get up and dig in. Don't view this storm as a stumbling block or a tombstone; instead see it as a steppingstone! We've been told to "Consider it pure joy when you face trials of many kinds, because the testing of your faith develops perseverance" (James 1:2-3, NIV).

Being an athlete, I try to view the discouraging times as the conditioning phase before the start of the season. You see, this is a time that no athlete enjoys, but they grin and bear it because they know that it's necessary. The tough practices and the pain are making them stronger, sharper, and better equipped to win. I went through a time of conditioning early in my network marketing business. In the first two weeks of my business:

- The product price went up about 35%, and the compensation plan changed structure completely.

- My best friend from high school told me, "No!" when I was counting on him to partner with me. And my father-in-law laughed in my face, because he thought the whole thing was a joke.

- I traveled three and a half hours to help a new distributor get their business started, but because the people they had invited to the event weren't able to make it, they didn't even show up... and forgot to call and tell me.

At the time, this was painful and discouraging.... But looking back, I can see now that it was just the conditioning before the season. It was tough, but it made me stronger, sharper, and better equipped to win. It taught me how to discipline my disappointments.

Discipline your Disappointments.

If you want to be a winner, you must know how to discipline your disappointments. You must always remain adaptable and adjustable. If you don't wake up every day excited about your future, then you need to identify what is stealing your happiness. If it's the thought of the painful day ahead, change your perspective. View it as the conditioning phase before the season, a necessary training session setting you up for a big win. Train your mind to see the good and be grateful for all that you have. When you get out of bed in the morning, put a smile on your face. Set the tone right at the start of the day. Understand that if you don't set the tone, someone else will set it for you.

> **If you don't set the tone, someone else will set it for you.**

Expect to Win Big!

Author and speaker Chuck Swindoll noted:

Excellence requires 100% all of the time. If you doubt that, try maintaining excellence by setting your standards at 92%. Or even 95%. People figure they're doing fine so long as they get somewhere near it. Excellence gets reduced to acceptable, and before long, acceptable doesn't seem worth the sweat if you can get by with adequate. After that, mediocrity is only a breath away! Lack of excellence has nothing to do with talent, personality, conditions, or luck. Excellence is always a choice. More importantly, we cannot live in a way that is inconsistent with our expectations for ourselves.[7]

To illustrate my point about having high expectations, I often tell the story of a man who approached a Little League baseball game one afternoon. He asked a boy in the dugout what the score was. The boy responded, "Eighteen to nothing — we're behind." "Boy," said the spectator, "I'll bet you're discouraged." "Why should I be discouraged?" replied the little boy. "We haven't even gotten up to bat yet!"

Expect Excellence!

You see, no matter what situation you are currently in, you must keep your expectations high in order to increase your odds of winning. When all the cards seem to be stacked

22

against you, it is in that moment that you must refuse to let negative thoughts, pessimism, and doubt creep into your mind and poison your ATTITUDE. The bottom line on ATTITUDE is that a *good one* helps to increase your possibilities. Pessimists usually get what they expect. So do optimists. Believing in yourself increases your chances of success. Take responsibility for your ATTITUDE, expect to win big, and expect excellence.

Wear the Right Cologne or Perfume!

The most influential person you'll talk to all day long is you. If you are constantly saying critical things about yourself internally, you won't be confident with yourself or with others.

In my school teaching days, and still now, I set it as a top priority to help others see and embrace their gifts. I do this because I know what the power of self-confidence can do in helping people overcome adversity and achieve big goals. Do not doubt yourself, because anywhere doubt resides, confidence cannot. Be confident in who you are! I love the joke about the man who was the mayor of his city. He was riding on a float with his wife in a parade down Main Street. At one point he spotted his wife's former boyfriend, who happened to be the owner of the local gas station. He snickered and whispered to his wife, "Aren't you glad you didn't marry him? You'd be working at a gas station!" The wife looked over at her husband and said, "Oh, honey, if I had married him, *he'd* be the mayor!" Just like the mayor's wife, we should exude confidence. Just like our cologne or perfume, we should spray it on every morning so that people can smell it anytime they come in contact with us.

I was speaking at a new market event with a lot of folks who had never seen me present before. At the end of the presentation, one man stood up and thanked me, but then said, "You know... we thought you would be taller." That got a good laugh because I was smaller than they'd thought I would be. Jokingly he threw another jab, "I wanna know, Chris, just how much do you weigh?" I smiled and said, "I'm 165 pounds of pure steel."

My question to you is, "What kind of cologne or perfume are you wearing today?" If you are sporting the scent of self-doubt, you have undercut your odds of succeeding before you even begin. I choose to give myself an immediate competitive advantage by spraying on my "confidence cologne." You should do the same. Remind yourself of the skills and attributes that you possess, not the ones you lack.

> **What kind of cologne are you wearing today?**

AFFIRMATIONS!

Which Wolf Are You Feeding?

An old Cherokee tale tells of a grandfather teaching life principles to his grandson. The wise old man said, "Son, on the inside of every person a battle is raging between two wolves. One wolf is evil. It's angry, jealous, unforgiving, proud, and lazy. The other wolf is good. It's filled with love, kindness, humility, and self-control. These two wolves are constantly fighting," the grandfather said. The little boy thought about it and said, "Grandfather, which wolf is going to win?" The grandfather smiled and said, "Whichever one you feed." My question to you is, which wolf are you feeding?[8]

> **Which wolf are you feeding?**

Affirm What You Want!

There are many scientific studies that have been done to prove the power of affirmation. To me, the word affirmation refers to whatever reality we speak into our lives and believe to be true. Whether positive or negative, our words and thoughts have a huge impact on our ability to succeed. An overwhelming majority of these studies prove that those who believed they could improve or succeed did.

The mind is a powerful thing. I was blown away by some evidence in the book, *The Happiness Advantage*, by Shawn Achor. It validates the statement, *what we think about, we bring about*. One study showed that placebos are about 55 to 60 percent as effective as most active medications like aspirin and codeine for controlling pain.

How can this be? It's a simple change in mindset and belief, and it's powerful enough to make the symptoms actually disappear. A second study in Shawn Achor's book highlighted what might be thought of as the reverse placebo effect, which is in many ways even more fascinating.

Japanese researchers blindfolded a group of students and told them their right arms were being rubbed with a poison ivy plant. Afterward, all 13 of the students' arms reacted with the classic symptoms of poison ivy: itching, boils, and redness. Not surprising until you find out that the plant used for the study wasn't poison ivy at all, just a harmless shrub. The students' beliefs were actually strong enough to create the biological effects of poison ivy, even though no such plant had touched them. Then, on the students' other arm, the researchers rubbed actual poison ivy, but told them it was a harmless plant. Even though all 13 students were highly allergic, only two of them broke out into the poison ivy rash.[9]

Have a Pep Rally!

If I were you — and I'm not you, but if I were you — and I knew that there were scientific studies out there that proved that *what you think about, you bring about*, I would be looking in the mirror having a pep rally for myself every morning. Maybe what you've been doing is working out great for you. You roll out of bed with complaints and pessimism, dreading the work ahead of you for the day because even though you may say it, you don't really believe that your best days are just ahead.

Friend, please stop and listen. What if by simply giving yourself a pep talk each morning and speaking favor into your life, you could have more, be more, do more, and give more? What if by having a positive ATTITUDE about life and by taking the first bite out of your A.P.P.L.E. each day you could have favor and increase in your life and in your business?

> **What you think about, you bring about.**

I can personally testify to the power of a positive ATTITUDE and the power of affirming greatness by speaking words of encouragement into your life. I have used a practice that I like to call "Planting Seeds of Increase" for as long I can remember. While playing college baseball I would introduce my teammates to others using their goals for the season as their title.

"I'd like you to meet my buddy, <u>future conference player of the year</u>, John Doe!"

The season might not have even started yet, but I knew that I was planting a seed of increase that, if watered and nurtured with confidence, would produce whatever fruit they desired.

When I coached middle school basketball, in my early teaching days, if I ran into one of my players in the hallway, I'd ask them about their day by calling them not only by name, but by the potential I saw in them.

"Jane Doe, how's the <u>top rebounder in tonight's game</u> doing today?"

Even in my early network marketing days, when a business partner and I would have accountability calls, we would start off by calling each other by the future rank that we aspired to hold.

"Good morning, John — going Diamond Elite — Doe!"

In all three real life examples given above, you should know... the prophecies came true.

Plant Seeds of Increase!

So right now, think of some people in your life that you can plant seeds of increase in. They can be your family, your friends, or your business partners. What words can you use to speak greatness into them? Take time each week to water the seeds of increase and help confidence grow. You may think it sounds silly, you may think it's stupid... but there are studies out there to prove its effectiveness, and I'm telling you it's worked like a charm for me.

> **Think of some people you can plant seeds of increase in.**

Seeds of increase...

What's Your Commercial?

Every morning I like to assess my ATTITUDE. I do this by giving myself what Zig Ziglar calls a "check up from the neck up!"[10] I'm a smack talker by nature, especially when in competition against myself. Each morning I like to start by smack talking myself with one   of my favorite quotes:

"Somewhere he is out there training while I am not,
and when we meet he will win."
-Mike Krzyzewski (Coach K)

That quote fires me up enough to get my behind out of the bed! Then I speak favor and increase into my own life by quoting the following:

> *"I'm a beast, I'm a winner, I'm strong, I'm courageous, I'm confident. I will have favor and increase today. I will be a blessing and be blessed today. So get your HOPES up, Estes!"*

That's my personal commercial; every morning I sell myself to myself. I use my words to bless my day. I plant seeds of increase into my own life. Remember, you must see value IN yourself to add value TO yourself. What does your commercial look like? Would you buy into you? I can guarantee that if you don't believe your hype, if you don't buy into yourself, no one else will either. Take a moment right now to write your own commercial, plant seeds of increase for yourself.

Personal Commercial...

Put your commercial in a place that you visit so routinely you can't help but read it multiple times a day. Whether that's on your car dashboard or your bathroom mirror, resolve to read it out loud several times throughout the day until you have it memorized, until it becomes a part of you. The key is that over time, the seeds of increase you are planting in your life will grow and produce fruits of success most people can only dream of.

Attitude points to remember...

- It's a choice.

- Choose now!

- You have everything you need!

- It's not always sunshine and rainbows!

- Affirmations!

  o Plant seeds of increase

  o Personal commercial

2

a.P.p.l.e.

"P" stands for PREPARE

*"The game is won before the game is begun, if you
understand the process!"*
- John C. Maxwell

The Good Life

Let me take you back to the summer of 2008. I was a full
time P.E. teacher and coach for a small town public school
system. I had coached everything under the sun: tennis,
baseball, basketball, the jump rope team, and even the cup-
stacking club. Don't laugh — those are all facts. Each day
after practice I kept my athletic hat on and went straight into
training for my own competitions. You see, I was also big into
triathlons: swim, cycle, run. Once the workout was complete,
I would retire to my house to shower, eat, and park my
backside for the night on the couch to watch a lot of mind-
numbing reality TV. I thought this was the good life, I thought
I had arrived! No, I didn't have much money in the bank, but
most of the time I had enough to get by. I never stopped to
really consider anything too far into the future. I was just
running on auto pilot... have you ever felt like that?

I have since learned that people's lives change every 60 to 90 days — whether they plan for them to or not. Two things happened that summer that completely altered the course of my life.

> **People's lives change every 60 to 90 days — whether they plan for them to or not.**

First, I found out my first child was on the way. Talk about not being PREPARED and feeling the pressure. Scared to death, I was 30 but felt like I was 18. All I could think about was, "How am I going to afford a baby? What do you even do with a baby? What should I expect?" With all these questions, I did the only thing a grown man could do... I called my momma. All in all, this news hit me like a ton of bricks. I was not at home much, due to my commitments with the various teams I was coaching and my training schedule. How was I going to find the time to be home long enough to help raise a child? I knew that if I didn't change some things I was going to spend my life raising other people's kids, but was never going to see my own.

The summer of 2008 was also when a friend introduced me to an opportunity in the profession of network marketing. I had heard of network marketing over the years and had even been introduced to one opportunity in my college apartment living room when I was 19. At that time in my life I was focused on other things; I was playing college baseball, majoring in girls, and living off of my parents. I never took a genuine look or investigated the benefits of that particular company, or network marketing in general. It just wasn't the right time in my life, so I passed on the opportunity without a second thought. In 2008, however, the timing was right... In fact, I was desperate. I was like a rattlesnake that had been backed into a corner; ready to fight my way out of the situation I was in.

Inspiration or Desperation?

I have found that people take action in life, and especially in network marketing, for one of two reasons: out of inspiration or desperation. I was acting out of desperation. The network marketing company I was introduced to was not my first choice in life, but it was my last chance. It was my last chance to really change the trajectory of my family's future and do something great. Yes, I threw up many roadblocks as to why I couldn't get started and make a change. Yes, I said I didn't have the money. Yes, I said I didn't have the time. Yes, I said I didn't know enough people. Yes, I said I had never been in business. But, what I learned is something that Jim Rohn said: "If you really want to do something, you'll find a way. If you don't, you'll find an excuse." All you need is one good reason to win, and you will overcome every excuse you can come up with. I took the advice of Abe Lincoln, who said, "Good things may come to those who wait, but only the things left by those who hustle."

Ready to Hustle.

The timing in 2008 couldn't have been any better, so I took a genuine look at the company. I saw a lot of value in the products and wanted to use them myself. As a triathlete, I was always looking for an edge on my competition. But, considering my growing family now, I was even more intrigued by the business opportunity. The news of my daughter's upcoming arrival had forced me to examine my financial situation and I realized that I wanted more for her than what I currently had, which was a full-time job and a part-time life.

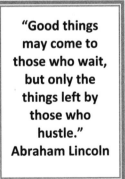

"Good things may come to those who wait, but only the things left by those who hustle."
Abraham Lincoln

I made a decision to get started, and in a couple of years working my business part-time, I was able to build a residual income that in some months exceeded what I had been making in a year with traditional employment. I know it's hard to believe, right? Believe it: that's the power of network marketing.

You might think that this is the point where I got all my ducks in a row and figured my life out... then sailed smoothly from there on. WRONG! This was just the beginning of the most unbalanced time of my life. Why? Because, I had no idea how to PREPARE my days to maintain production *and* balance. Every spare moment I had was now geared toward growing my new venture.

Unbalanced...

Over the course of the next several months, I did very little other than work the business. I was constantly on the road and "in the trenches," as it is referred to in the network marketing profession. I no longer took time at all for the things that used to consume my time. I even stopped doing the things that were important to me, the things that brought me joy and fulfillment. Why? Because I didn't understand how to PREPARE my schedule to accommodate progress professionally *and* personally. I was gaining success in one area at the expense of everything else. I was afraid of slowing down because I didn't want to lose momentum with the business, but I was concerned that the neglect in all the other aspects of my life would eventually catch up to me. And it did.

> I didn't understand how to PREPARE my schedule to accommodate progress professionally *and* personally.

As business boomed I exercised less and less and ate out more and more. Sundays were rarely a day of rest for me and, regrettably, rarely a day of worship. I was home more with my family during the day, but only physically; mentally I was working. Something had to change.

Thankfully, network marketing is a profession that promotes service to others in the form of mentoring. I was fortunate enough to gain the mentorship of Paul Orberson, a man who had been where I currently was. Paul had seen rapid growth in his business like I was seeing in mine; he knew what was ahead for me — the good and the challenging. He advised me to take back control of my life, to PREPARE my days for success. Paul said that either you run the day, or the day will run you; you own your time, or time will own you.

> "Either you run the day, or the day will run you; you own your time, or time will own you."
> —Paul Orberson

Road Map for the Journey.

I met with as many mentors as I could. I asked them multiple questions about their daily agendas and how they were able to attain balance in their personal life AND momentum in their business all at the same time. Each time that question would bring a chuckle, as none of them had mastered having balance and momentum fully. However, they all gave me some clues on how to get better, how to have more balance than I currently had. I took all of the advice, sorted through it and mixed it with my own beliefs, and finally had a breakthrough.

It was a big day in my life when I realized that it was possible to win any game that I set out to play if I would simply PREPARE to win. It was a big "A HA" for me to really understand, and truly believe, that huge goals could be reached in multiple areas of my life if I would just be very intentional and deliberate in mapping out my days. After that, I was determined to live my life on purpose and with balance. Thus the creation of my life's plan.

I can't emphasize to you enough how I wish I would have had this "A HA" moment at the start of my business. Not only would a Life Plan have sped up the success; it would have also saved multiple other areas of my life from the stress and strain brought on by my negligence. In his book *The Slight Edge*, Jeff Olson put it this way: "It's never too late to start. It's always too late to wait."[1] You can start now. Create a Life Plan and eat your A.P.P.L.E. everyday.

THE POWER OF PREPARATION!

Take Bite #2

The second bite of the A.P.P.L.E. that I eat everyday stands for the word PREPARE. When you PREPARE, you are putting yourself in a better position to succeed; you're positioning yourself to be effective with your time. As Solomon wrote in the book of Proverbs, "The plans of the diligent lead to profit as surely as haste leads to poverty" (Proverbs 21:5, NLT). Haste is a synonym for words such as urgency and speedy action... all good when it's time to implement your plan, but not so much when you're creating it. I lived in a small town in Kentucky: Hodgenville, the birthplace of Abraham Lincoln. Now good ol' Abe said, "Give me six hours to chop down a tree and I will spend the first four sharpening the axe." You see, time spent PREPARING for the journey clears the road and makes for smoother travel.

> "It's never too late to start. It's always too late to wait."
> —Jeff Olson

Preparation Relieves Pressure!

If you win, it's because you understand that there is an entire process before the day you win. I have observed the truth to that statement over the past few years. My experience has led me to see that super achievers enjoy the journey toward success just as much as, if not more than, they do the actual destination. Those who win do so because they value the process of winning. I want to encourage you to embrace the process of winning because PREPARATION relieves pressure.

As I mentioned in the chapter on attitude, I once traveled three and a half hours to help a new distributor get their business started. Then, because the people they had invited to the event weren't able to make it, they didn't even show up or bother to call and let me know. This caused major pressure to build up in my head; so much so that I thought I might explode. I took the long car ride home as an opportunity to reflect. I began to question myself, "Chris, what good is whining about this doing anyone?" I made a decision to stop sucking my thumb and instead view the situation with a winning attitude. I chose to view the drive not as a loss, but as a learning experience. And I learned to be PREPARED for that situation to happen again. Now, I travel with several personal development CD's in hand, turning my vehicle into a drive-time university so that if I arrive and no one else does, I can still view the trip as a win. What did I win? I just won several hours of personal development time that I would otherwise have not gotten. Regardless of what you do as a profession, or what your daily agenda looks like, it's always a good idea to PREPARE for the unexpected pop quizzes, hope for and expect the best, and find the positive spin in every situation. Remember, PREPARATION relieves pressure.

> **PREPARATION**
> **relieves**
> **pressure.**

Practice Makes You.

After his retirement, John Wooden, a ten-time NCAA National Championship basketball coach at UCLA, was asked what he missed most about the game; he said practice. He said by the time the game came, he was so relaxed that he could just sit on the bench, roll up his program, and enjoy the show. It was already a done deal. He said the game had to be played to make it official in the books, but it was already done. In other words, John Wooden understood the process; he knew that the game is won before the game has begun. That is the power of PREPARATION.

HAVE A LIFE PLAN!

Get In The Game!

Not many people give extensive thought to the details of their life journey. I would speculate that even fewer actually have a detailed written plan for their life and for where they want to be in one, three, or five years from today. Let's face it, most people just resort to watching their life play out as it may, moment by moment. They choose to sit in the stands and watch, even though this is their game to play. We have all heard of New Year's Resolutions; many people consider that their planning for the year. This is very unfortunate, since a vast majority of New Year's Resolutions are broken before the end of January. Now, I don't think that this is a conscious choice; it's just that it has never crossed some people's minds to make a real plan for their life. A plan for vacation and a plan for the weekend everyone seems to understand, but a Life Plan is too far-fetched for most. The result of sitting in the stands watching instead of getting in the game is full-on regret. People end up discouraged, asking, "Where did I go wrong?" How do I know that this is the question that most people will ask at some point in their life? Because it was the question I asked myself. That was the question before I took control of my future, before I harnessed the power of a Life Plan.

> It has never crossed some people's minds to make a real plan for their life.

WHAT'S YOUR DEFINITION OF SUCCESS?

What Does Success Mean?

The vision I now had was like a breath of fresh air. It seemed like such a no-brainer thing to do... to make a plan for my life. I kept asking myself, "Why haven't I been doing this for the past ten years?" But, this was the first time I had ever really sat down and systematically thought about what I wanted on a big-picture scale. It boiled down to asking myself this simple question:

What does success mean to me?

This is a powerful question that I would encourage you to ask yourself: What would success look like in your life? Do you have it now? If not, are you willing to make some changes in order to have it in the future? My hope is that you will let me coach you through the process that I went through to get from a place of complacency in my own life, to a life unlimited.

> **This is a powerful question that I would encourage you to ask yourself: What would success look like in your life?**

Just Three Steps!

It takes a lot of deep thought to answer that question, but it was easier when I simplified it down to three basic steps:

1. Identify your Buckets and your WHY.
2. Commit your goals to paper and set deadlines.
3. Create an Action Plan.

STEP 1 - IDENTIFY YOUR BUCKETS and YOUR WHY!

Identify your Buckets!

What Areas Are Most Important To You?

You may be wondering, "Now Chris, how do you even begin the process of planning for success or creating a Life Plan?" For me, the first step in getting my life back on track and headed toward the destination of my choosing was to identify where it was that I wanted to go. What did success look like for me? I can tell you, this is a much tougher question than one might think. Sure, I wanted to own my own time... Yes, I wanted to have choices and options... Absolutely, I wanted to leave a legacy for my family by adding value to people. But, those desires were all too broad to put into action. Once I was forced to dig deep, to get through the fog of the complex and back to the clarity of the simple, I realized that I wanted these things not just with my finances, not just in my network marketing business, but in several other areas of my life. We all want success, and we want it alongside a balanced and fulfilling WHOLE life. So how do we get that? We get it by first identifying all of the areas of our life that are important to us; the areas in which we want to feel accomplished. These areas I like to call the Buckets of my life.

It just happened to work out that all of my Buckets begin with the same sound, but even in Kentucky we know they don't start with the same letter.

My BUCKETS:

Faith
Family
Finance
Fitness
Food
Fun
Philanthropy

You have to decide for yourself what areas, or Buckets, in your life deserve detailed attention. Identifying the Buckets is the first step in becoming an active participant in your life, intentionally shaping your own future. Take a few minutes right now to jot down the areas of your life that are most important to you. Identify your Buckets.

 Identify your BUCKETS:

If this is your first time ever creating a plan for your life, all of this may seem overwhelming for you. If that's the case, I would encourage you to start with a small bite. Of the Buckets that you listed, choose just one for now to focus on. I would suggest it be your Finance Bucket, and more specifically, your network marketing business.

Identify your WHY!

Why Do You Want It?

The second half of Step One in creating your Life Plan is determining your motivation for wanting success in the Buckets that you have identified. What are the reasons why you want what you want in your life? Your WHY has to be strong enough to hold you accountable to the commitments you are making to your future. I believe Darren Hardy said it best in his book, *The Compound Effect*, when he said, "Commitment is doing the thing you said you would do, long after the mood you said it in has left you." Your WHY has to be strong enough to keep you committed when it gets frustrating, when it gets hard, and when it gets downright painful. You see, when you find your WHY, you find your

41

way. When I do trainings on *WHY Power* for my network marketing business I like to use the illustration below:

> *Pretend you are on the rooftop of a skyscraper. Imagine a wooden plank placed between your rooftop and another one just a few feet away. Your task is to walk on that wooden plank from your skyscraper roof across to the other side. Your reward for taking action is $100 bill, but if you fall it would mean certain death.*
>
> *I am going to guess that not many of you would be motivated to risk your life walking the plank for $100.*
>
> *Now, let's picture a different scenario. Let's say that you are on that same skyscraper with the same wooden plank separating the roof you are on from the other just a few feet away. Only this time, on the second skyscraper instead of money is your child... and the roof they are on is on fire.*
>
> *Every one of us just sprinted across that plank without a moment's hesitation.*

This is how strong your motivation has to be. If your WHY doesn't make you cry, it isn't strong enough.

In the beginning of my network marketing career, I found

> **If your WHY doesn't make you cry, it isn't strong enough.**

my WHY in the love and overwhelming responsibility I felt toward a child I'd not even met yet. I was determined that my daughter would have more than I currently had, would have the best opportunities, and would not be raised by strangers while I raised other people's kids. What is your WHY?

Take a moment right now to determine the reason WHY you want more than you currently have.

Are You Willing To Pay The Price?

What price will you be willing to pay to obtain your version of success? For some the cost will be much greater than it is for others; that's just the way it is. The amount of time it takes will vary from case to case as well. In most instances it's not who wants it the most, but rather who wants it the longest and who is willing to stay committed. According to Zig Ziglar, "The major difference between the big shot and the little shot is the big shot is just a little shot who kept on shooting."[2]

Pay or Play?

The old fable of the ant and the grasshopper explains this concept so well. You see, the grasshopper spent his time in the warm months hopping, chirping, and singing until his little heart was content; never once giving thought to the cold months ahead. The ant, on the other hand, spent the warm months gathering food and PREPARING for winter. Then that season arrived, as it always does, and the grasshopper found himself dying of hunger and begging for food. In the end, this fable just reminds us of something that John Maxwell often says: "You can pay now and play later OR play now and pay later; either way, you are going to have to pay."

Stick and Stay!

Paul Orberson used to tell me, "Chris, if you'll stick and stay, you'll get your pay." The Bible has several different testimonies of men who were truly committed to "sticking and staying." After all, God likes to PREPARE people in crockpots, not in microwaves.

- Noah – waited 120 years for the rain
- Abraham – waited 25 years for his promised son
- Joseph – waited 14 years in prison for a crime he didn't commit
- Job – waited a lifetime for God's justice

Commitment or Interest?

Please know that there is a big difference between commitment and interest. When you are interested in doing something, you do it only when it's convenient. When you are committed to doing something, you accept no excuses. I want to encourage you to stick and stay, to pay the price, and to stand firm in commitment to your goals and dreams. I'm not saying it will be easy, but I can assure you that it will be worth it. Like my friend and mentor John Maxwell says, "Hoping for a good future without investing in today is like a farmer waiting for a harvest without ever planting any seed." I want to encourage you to stop wishing for your dreams to come true and instead PREPARE for them to.

> **Stop wishing for your dreams to come true and instead PREPARE for them to.**

STEP 2 – COMMIT YOUR GOALS TO PAPER and SET DEADLINES!

Start Small!

In Step 1 we identified the Buckets of our life that deserve high attention and found a strong WHY to hold us accountable. I want to stop here and reiterate that if you are new to the life planning process, it may be advantageous to only create goals in your FINANCE Bucket and your network marketing business at this time. Maybe planning and organizing are not natural strengths for you, and that's okay. They were not for me when I started, and still today, by no means am I a master organizer. But, through intentionality and *The A.P.P.L.E. Principle* I have been able to improve over time, bringing huge progress in my life and network marketing business. So please know that this is not an "all or nothing" process. You can start with whatever size bite feels comfortable to you; the key is just that you START.

> **You can start with whatever size bite feels comfortable to you; the key is just that you START.**

Bite by Bite...

Keep in mind, though, that the principle applies to all areas of your life. Once you get the hang of it in your network marketing business you can come back to your Buckets and choose another area of your life to apply *The A.P.P.L.E. Principle* to. Moving forward, I will be giving you examples from multiple Buckets of my life so that if you're a veteran planner, you can expand your Life Plan. I will then go into further detail on the network marketing examples for those of you who are just starting the life planning process. Again, if this is all new for you, and you have already completed Step 1, you have just set yourself up for a game-changing year. I want to encourage you to keep working through these steps because you're doing what most people will never do... and that, my friend, is called an advantage.

Brainstorm!

In Step 2 we will determine what specific goals we want to achieve in each of the Buckets of our lives, and then decide the deadline by which we want to achieve them. It's time to brainstorm. You have to do what works for you, but when I went through this process I wrote down everything that came to mind. Understand that what you are writing down are *your* goals and *your* dreams. The pen and paper will not judge or mock you. Mine was not an organized plan in the beginning; instead, it was a work in progress that had to be revised and revisited several times before the final copy was drafted. Make your goals so specific, so simple, that it is hard for you to talk yourself out of reaching them. Also, BEWARE: As Jim Rohn said, "We must be careful not to let our current appetites steal away any chance we might have for a future feast." This will be very hard to do considering that we live in an instant gratification society. You have to continually tell yourself to think long-range and big-picture goals, yet in simple terms.

Courtside Seats.

Let me give you an example: I love watching University of Kentucky sporting events, especially UK Basketball. Inside of my FUN Bucket I had a goal to see every game and every play live and up close, not on TV and not from the top of the stadium. I wanted to sit so close that I could smell the sweat. Since I knew that I couldn't expect courtside seats by putting in nosebleed efforts, I chose to pay the price up front. I chose the future feast. The first year of my network marketing business, I missed every single ballgame on TV. I went to business presentations instead. To be quite honest with you, I pretty much gave up three entire seasons of watching UK Basketball because I was determined not to let my current appetite at the time steal my center-court season tickets for life. Figure out what you really want, because you can have it if you are willing to pay the price.

BUCKET:	GOAL (YEAR 3):
Fun	Center court season tickets

46

Aim High!

The hardest part of goal setting is getting past your current reality into what is your potential future reality. Society has herded us all into thinking that the really good stuff in life is only for those who get lucky or have freakish gifts or talents from birth. Don't believe that lie. We all have, at this very moment, everything that we need to get to anywhere we want to go. Don't sell your future short because of your current lack of vision. Aim high and think big for your life. As the great artist Michelangelo said, "The greatest danger for most of us is not that our aim is too high and we miss it, but that our aim is too low and we reach it."

Raise Your Sights!

I heard a story several years ago that validates the message of aiming high. In the story, a shepherd's son has come of age and goes out to spend his first summer alone tending the sheep in the hills above the village. One night, he awakens to the sound of a wolf howling nearby. The night is black and he is seized by fear, but he dutifully grabs his rifle and races out into the darkness to protect his livestock. Across the way

> "The greatest danger for most of us is not that our aim is too high and we miss it, but that our aim is too low and we reach it."
> —Michelangelo

he sees a wolf at the throat of one of the sheep. As he puts his rifle to his shoulder and takes aim, he remembers the advice of his father: "At night, it is very difficult to judge the distance to your target, and more than likely, you'll underestimate the distance and miss low. To have a better chance of hitting the target, aim high." The shepherd's son adjusts his aim, raising the sights ever so slightly, and hits the mark.

You may have voices telling you that you've already missed your shot... that it's never going to happen for you. WRONG! The advice that I share at speaking engagements and to those that I personally mentor and coach is to not sell yourself short. Aim high and get your hopes up — knowing, believing, and expecting that no matter what your current situation or location, your best days are just ahead.

Here are a few additional examples of my brainstorming. Use it to spark some thoughts for yourself.

BUCKET:	GOAL (YEAR 1):
Faith	Read entire Bible
Family	Maddie/Daddy date 1/month
Finance • Network Marketing	Connect with 1300 people inside my organization

Take time right now to decide what you want in the different Buckets of your life, or just in your network marketing business for starters. Think big and aim high; don't be afraid to write down what you actually want, no matter how far-fetched it may seem. Be encouraged that if you can see your goal, you're moving toward it. On the other hand, if you can't see it, you're NOT.

Paul Orberson always told me to go as far as I could see, and when I got there I would be able to see farther. Now you may be thinking, "Chris, I just can't imagine being able to accomplish such big goals. I just can't see myself being that blessed." Can I tell you something? If you can't see yourself accomplishing that big goal or being that blessed, then there is no need to worry, because it won't happen for you. So I want to encourage you to START. That way you CAN see something and begin to move toward it... so it WILL happen.

BUCKET:	GOAL (YEAR 1):

BUCKET:	GOAL (YEAR 3):

BUCKET:	GOAL (YEAR 5):

If looking three and five years out seems too unreachable for you, just start with one Bucket and one year goals in that Bucket. You can always expand on it later.

Commit Your Goals To Paper!

It's Time To Organize!

Now that we have brainstormed and come up with some lofty goals in each of our Buckets (or just our network marketing business) that span one, three, and possibly even five years out; it's time to organize. This is where your actual

Life Plan starts to form. You see, until you commit your goals to paper, you have intentions that are seeds without soil. But when you get them planted, or clearly stated on paper, that is when they start to grow and become your reality. As an added bonus, this is also when you jolt yourself into a very elite group. In his book *Success Principles*, Jack Canfield said that studies show that being clear about your purpose, vision, and goals puts you in the top 3% of the world's achievers.[3]

Join the 3%

Why do so few create a Life Plan? Because the process of goal setting is very demanding. In fact, that is the reason only 3% of people write goals down and create a plan for their life. It is also one reason the rewards for those who do are so great. Let me repeat that: ONLY 3% OF PEOPLE WRITE THEIR GOALS DOWN. I am a competitor by nature, so knowing that I can get ahead of 97% by simply creating a plan for my life just adds fuel to my fire. You might be saying, "Now Chris, I just don't have the time right now." If that is the case, let me pose this question: If you don't have time to invest in establishing a written Life Plan, is it possible that you don't have time because you don't have a written Life Plan? In all probability, lack of time always has been and always will be the problem.

It's Nothing Fancy!

My official Life Plan is nothing fancy, just a good ol' Excel spread sheet with six columns across the top:

- Bucket
- Goal
- Deadline
- Action Plan
- How I will measure my progress
- When I will do the action plan

the A.P.P.L.E.

Chris D. Estes — *Principle*

Life Plan

BUCKET	GOAL (1 YEAR)	DEADLINE	ACTION PLAN	HOW MEASURED	WHEN DONE

WWW.THEAPPLEPRINCIPLE.COM

Remember, *The A.P.P.L.E. Principle* applies to all Buckets in your Life Plan. To start, let's focus on inserting only the amount of Buckets we can handle with confidence at this time, and then the goals that we have set in those Buckets. My hope is that you will see the power of this principle as we walk through this process together, bite by bite, and over time you will build on this foundation.

Life Plan

BUCKET	GOAL (1 YEAR)	DEADLINE	ACTION PLAN	HOW MEASURED	WHEN DONE
FAITH	READ ENTIRE BIBLE				
FAMILY	12 MADDIE/DADDY DATES				
FINANCE	CONNECT WITH 1300 PEOPLE				

51

Set Deadlines!

Deadlines Hold You Accountable!

Without giving deadlines to your vision, your vision may end up dead. Procrastination is the name of the game for most people. Heck, that was my middle name for a while. As a standard, 80% of the work to complete any project is done in the last 20% of the time allotted. The words tomorrow, today, and the end of the month are not on calendars for a reason. We must state the exact date by which we want to have achieved our goal.

Life Plan

BUCKET	GOAL (1 YEAR)	DEADLINE	ACTION PLAN	HOW MEASURED	WHEN DONE
FAITH	READ ENTIRE BIBLE	12/31			
FAMILY	12 MADDIE/DADDY DATES	12/31			
FINANCE	CONNECT WITH 1300 PEOPLE	12/31			

STEP 3 – CREATE AN ACTION PLAN!

Chart the Course!

Now that we know where we want to go and when we want to arrive, we have to chart our course to get there. What actions must be taken every day, every week, and every month to keep us in forward movement toward our goals? We will dive deeper into the topic of taking action and performing in the next chapter, but let's go ahead and set the stage. To insure progress, we should name the specific actions that need to be taken on a consistent basis and how we will measure our progress, and then decide when we will take these actions. To make creating the Action Plan for your goals as simple as possible, we will follow the three steps below:

3 STEPS FOR CREATING AN ACTION PLAN:

1. Work backward from the long-range goal until you have the action broken into its smallest bite (daily, weekly, or monthly action).
2. Know how you will measure your progress or keep track of when you do or do not take that small bite (daily, weekly, or monthly action).
3. Decide specifically when you are going to take that small bite (daily, weekly, or monthly action).

1. Work Backward

How Do You Eat An Elephant?

To work backward, we must begin with the end in mind. Once we establish our long-range goal, we then break it down into smaller pieces (eg: five-year goal into five different one-year goals). After all, how do you eat an elephant? The same way you eat an A.P.P.L.E.: one bite at a time. These small pieces make the big goal more manageable. Once we identify what actions need to be taken in each of the 1-year pieces, we slice it even thinner: into four quarters (i.e. three-month segments).

This process repeats: the quarters into months, the months into weeks, the weeks into days, and the days into hours and sometimes minutes. What does this mean? It means that we now have broken down, bite by bite, our five-year goal that seemed too big and impossible, into small daily actions. These smaller bites are much easier to swallow. Your Action Plan must be very specific and extremely simple to carry out and measure.

So Simple...

For example, if you have a goal in your FINANCE Bucket to read 12 books on finance in a year you will have to work backward from that long-range goal to come up with your Action Plan.

YEAR BROKEN INTO MONTH:

12 books ÷ 12 months in a year = 1 book each month

MONTH BROKEN INTO DAY:

Total pages in the book ÷ Total days in the month = Total pages read each day

EXAMPLE:

150-page book ÷ 30 days in the month = 5 pages each day

Then your Life Plan may look like this:

Life Plan

BUCKET	GOAL (1 YEAR)	DEADLINE	ACTION PLAN	HOW MEASURED	WHEN DONE
FINANCE	READ 12 BOOKS	12/31	READ 5 PAGES EACH DAY		

I have several different goals in each of my Buckets. I have given you just a few in the example from my Life Plan below.

Life Plan

BUCKET	GOAL (1 YEAR)	DEADLINE	ACTION PLAN	HOW MEASURED	WHEN DONE
FAITH	READ ENTIRE BIBLE	12/31	DAILY READING FOLLOWING OUTLINE FROM WWW.BIBLEYEAR.COM		
FAMILY	12 MADDIE/DADDY DATES	12/31	SCHEDULE DATE DAYS 3 MONTHS IN ADVANCE, LOCK IN ON MY CALENDAR		
FINANCE	CONNECT WITH 1300 PEOPLE	12/31	TOUCH 5 PROGRAM		

The Action Plan for my network marketing business Touch 5 Program will be explained in detail a little later in this chapter.

Create Your Own Syllabus!

Since I come from a background in education, I tried to think of each goal as a separate project that was due for a class. My Life Plan, in a sense, was a life syllabus. It was a syllabus to map out different short-term projects (daily actions) that needed to be completed in an ongoing fashion to insure that the final project (the yearly goal) was done on time and in a first-class manner. Now we have all seen the effect that procrastination has on the quality of a project. It may still allow you to get the job done, but it never produces your best result. The saying goes that an apple a day keeps the doctor away; it doesn't say eat 30 apples on the last day of each month. The best way that I have found to ensure that I produce first class results, to ensure that I reach my goals by the deadlines that I have set for myself, is to become a master at managing *myself* in the time that I have.

There Are Only 24 Hours in a Day!

No matter who you are, you only ever have 24 hours in a day. The difference that separates average achievers from super achievers is the utilization of those given hours. Super achievers have a heightened awareness of the value of time. They name the use of their time before the time arrives; every hour is allocated to a specific task that will help them progress toward their goals. Some hours are invested in growing their talents, some hours are invested toward growing their business, some hours are invested in building family relationships, and hopefully some hours are invested in their health and fitness. I have learned through experience just how important these hours are. Very few of super achievers' 24 hours are haphazardly spent, or even worse lost.

Use the Eraser!

If something sneaks onto your schedule that isn't a priority or a task that moves you closer to your goals, use your eraser and take it off. It is a powerful thing, to take back control of your life... and it can be done with the simplest little word, "No!" I'll give an example from my own life to prove the power of saying "NO" to more things so that you can say "YES" to the right   things.

Recently, during the writing of this book, I was asked to speak to a group of network marketing professionals. They offered a substantial fee for my time, training, and knowledge of the industry. Unfortunately, speaking for a fee was not a top priority for me at that time; completing this book was. Deviating from the plan I had made to hit my book deadlines would have required me to invest a lot of time in preparing for the event, not to mention the time lost due to travel... and just for a one time monetary fee. Remember, you can always make the money; just don't let the money make you. I chose to decline their offer (multiple offers actually) because I knew that in order to reach my goal I had to keep the "main thing" the main thing.

Be Intentional.

> **Remember, you can always make money; just don't let the money make you.**

When I allocate my time, I don't stop at PREPARING my year by the month, my month by the week, or my week by the day. I PREPARE my days by the hour, and on occasion in even smaller increments. As I grow older, I continue to value my time more and more. Now, every little "bite" of time I have is so precious to me that I try to be very aware of how I use it. The art of mastering time is a process and will require sacrifice and self-discipline, especially in the action stage. I can say this is a very important topic for me. I'm not the sharpest tool or the brightest bulb around, but I understand that I can use intentionality to my advantage, and you can too. I know that every morning I wake up with the same amount of time as everyone else, and that if I am intentional with that time over the days, weeks, months, and years, I'll be able to create something that will outlast me. And that is the ultimate goal, to create something that will leave a legacy and continue to add value to others long after I'm gone. You see, it's one thing to map out a perfect day, and another thing all together when it comes to executing it.

Don't minimize the importance of self-management. Without self-management, no time-management system will work for you. Besides, no one actually manages time. You can only manage yourself. The amount of time in hours, days, weeks, months, and years remains stable regardless of what you do or don't do. No matter how you plan your day, it will never be 30 hours long, only 24 hours.

> No one actually manages time. You can only manage yourself.

Be a Super Achiever.

The key that needs to be taken away from all of the time management talk is simply that everyone has the potential to be a super achiever, to accomplish any goal, to change and go in the direction of their choosing, as long as they begin with a plan. Everyone is different, but I have found that what works best for me is to focus on the main things first. Schedule time to work on the main things before anything else.

Put the Big Rocks First.

Stephen Covey tells the story in *First Things First* of attending a seminar in which the instructor pulled out a wide-mouth gallon jar. He sat it on the table next to some fist-sized rocks. "How many of these rocks do you think we can get in the jar?" he asked. The students made various guesses. The instructor then proceeded to fill the jar with the rocks. It looked like it was full. He asked the class, "Is this jar full?" Everyone looked at the jar and agreed that it was indeed full. He then reached under the table and pulled out a bucket of gravel. He then dumped the gravel into the jar. The gravel went in between all the little places left by the big rocks. Then he grinned and once more asked, "Is the jar full?"

By this time, the class was on to him. "Probably not," several of the students said. "'Good," he replied. He reached under the table and brought out a bucket of sand. He poured it into the jar. It went into all the spaces left by the big rocks and the gravel. Again, he asked the class, "Is this jar full?" "No," the class shouted. He said, "Good." He then grabbed a pitcher of water and poured almost a quart of water into the jar. Then he asked, "What's the point?" Someone said, "If you really work at it, you can always squeeze more stuff into your life." "No," the instructor responded. "That's not the point. The point is this: if you hadn't put these big rocks in first, would you ever have gotten any of them in?"

Prioritize your Priorities!

The big rocks in this story represent the main things, the most important tasks or actions you can take to move you closer to your goals. If you don't make room for them, or schedule them first, your time will be consumed by the tasks that are less important to the big picture. In essence, we must prioritize our priorities. Don't get caught saying, "I just ran out of time." or, "I just don't know where the time went." These are merely excuses that are preventing you from reaching your goals. Be proactive and re-evaluate how you're spending your time now. What are you trading your time for? Make sure you are trading your time for the things that matter most.

> **What are you trading your time for?**

Trade Up, Not Down.

We all trade our time for something. Time for money, time with the family for time at the office, time at the gym for time spent in front of the TV, time today for a better future. The key is to trade wisely.

I would like to take you through the process I go through to plan my days and share a few productivity tips that have helped me achieve some big goals with only the 24 hours that are allotted to us each day. My hope is that you will see the value in the process, adopt some into your daily routine, and over time you too will be able to create success that will long outlive you. After all, the ultimate goal is not to live forever, but to create a legacy that will.

Tools for Planning.

There are three main tools that I use consistently to plan my life and network marketing business:

A. Weekly Activity Tracker

B. Weekly To Do List

C. Daily Time Budget

Every activity that makes it onto any of these three tools stems directly from the plan that I have for my life. Very rarely do I do activities that don't move me closer to the goals that I have set for myself in the different Buckets of my life. I would encourage you to start doing the same. Start small and focus on the actions that move you closer to your goals.

2. Measure your Progress

The first step in creating the Action Plan was to work backward from our big goal until we have the action broken into its smallest bite (daily, weekly, or monthly action). The second step in creating the Action Plan is to know how we will measure our progress or keep track of when we do or do not take that smallest bite (daily, weekly, or monthly action.) The tool we will use to track our progress on most of our goals is the Weekly Activity Tracker.

A. Weekly Activity Tracker

WEEKLY ACTIVITY TRACKER

Activity	M	T	W	TH	F	ST	SN
FAITH							
FAMILY							
FINANCE							
FITNESS							
FOOD							
FUN							
PHILANTHROPY							

WWW.THEAPPLEPRINCIPLE.COM

Measure Your Progress!

The Weekly Activity Tracker is broken into the different Buckets and lists the activities that need to be done in each Bucket on a daily basis to keep forward progress. Again, if this is all new for you, the key is to simply start. Begin with your FINANCE Bucket and focus on your network marketing activities. But, just for an example, you may have seen that I have a FAITH goal to read the entire Bible in one year. I take that long-range goal and work backward, like we talked about, until I have what activity I need to do daily to achieve success. In this case, I have decided that in order to reach the one-year goal I need to read a little bit every day. *(The exact schedule I follow to know what passages to read every day is found at www.bibleyear.com)*

On my Weekly Activity Tracker, I simply write "Read Bible" and then each day it either gets a check mark or an X. Simply by having to mark something in the box you are holding yourself accountable to do the activity you said you were going to do. It is very important to have a way to track your progress. We will talk more about this in the chapter on "Evaluate."

Touch 5!

My network marketing business is a component that falls in my FINANCE Bucket. I have a one-year goal to talk individually, or connect, with 1,300 people inside my organization. Part of the Action Plan I've created to achieve that goal is to talk to five people a day, five days a week. It's a program that I have promoted to my business partners and dubbed *Touch 5*. The name of the game in life and especially in network marketing is building relationships. I make a point to *Touch* 5 people everyday. Each *touch* is a simple phone call where I reach into the organization to congratulate, encourage, and motivate existing business partners.

On my Weekly Activity Tracker under the FINANCE section I simply write *Touch 5*. What kind of impact could you have on your business or your life if you were to *Touch 5* people every day with some positive encouragement? I'm not great at math, but I'm pretty sure that five people, five days per week, would equal 100 people in four weeks. That would mean that each year you would have planted seeds of increase into 1,300 different people. Do you think that would make a difference? I believe so.

Prospect 3!

You may be new to network marketing and haven't built a large enough organization to implement the full *Touch 5* program just yet, so just touch one or two. But no matter the size of your organization, your focus should be to *Prospect 3* new people each day. If this is the case, you would simply write *Prospect 3* on your Weekly Activity Tracker under the FINANCE Bucket. At the end of each day you either give yourself a check mark or an X because either you prospected three new people or you didn't.

WEEKLY ACTIVITY TRACKER

Activity	M	T	W	TH	F	ST	SN
FAITH							
READ BIBLE							
FINANCE							
TOUCH 5							
PROSPECT 3							

Life Plan

BUCKET	GOAL (1 YEAR)	DEADLINE	ACTION PLAN	HOW MEASURED	WHEN DONE
FAITH	READ ENTIRE BIBLE	12/31	DAILY READING FOLLOWING OUTLINE FROM WWW.BIBLEYEAR.COM	ACTIVITY TRACKER	
FAMILY	12 MADDIE/DADDY DATES	12/31	SCHEDULE DATE DAYS 3 MONTHS IN ADVANCE, LOCK IN ON MY CALENDAR	RECORD DATES COMPLETED ON LIFE PLAN	
FINANCE	CONNECT WITH 1300 PEOPLE	12/31	TOUCH 5 PROGRAM	ACTIVITY TRACKER	

B. Weekly To Do List

Items on the Weekly To Do List are things that need to be done to progress toward the goals, broken into three categories: *Must Do's, Should Do's,* and *Could Do's.*

Must Do

Must Do items are the big rocks. These things stem from my Activity Tracker, but are described in greater detail. *Must Do's* take first priority on my schedule, followed by other Activity Tracker items. They are significant actions that must be taken in order to reach my goals. These things almost never get put off or pushed to a later time. I would like to say that they NEVER do, but that would be a tall tale. But 99% of the time, once they make it onto my schedule, I guard that time with my life. Again, if this is all new for you, start small by choosing just one action as your only *To Do* for now, just making sure that it is a *Must Do* item.

Expanding on my earlier example, one *Must Do* that I have associated with my network marketing business inside my FINANCE Bucket, is to *Touch 5* people each day. *Touch 5* is written on my Activity Tracker, but to hold myself accountable to real people I choose the names of the folks I'm going to be reaching out to that week in advance. I do this on Sunday night during a time I call *Sunday Prep*. *We will talk about Sunday Prep in detail in the chapter on "Evaluate."* This means that my *Must Do* list for the week will contain 25 names with phone numbers.

Freedom Your Way!

If your business is in a place where your main focus is to attract more people and more leaders, the big rock or *Must Do* for you should be to *Prospect 3* new people everyday. After all, as Rick Berger says, "Three a day brings freedom our way."[4] On our Activity Tracker, we will write *Prospect 3*, but on our To Do list under the *Must Do's* we will write the names of the people we will be prospecting that week. I know what you are thinking right now: "Can't I just see who I run into on Tuesday, and prospect them on the spot?" Well sure you can,

> "Three a day brings freedom our way."
> —Rick Berger

but my mentor Paul Orberson once told me that if it's not on your calendar, it doesn't exist. So, I would advise you to consider those people who you just run into to be a bonus in addition to the three people that you have intentionally chosen for each day that week. Don't leave your plan in fate's hand. The odds for following through on the Action Plan increase dramatically if you name real people and exact times to call them. Try it. Be intentional and get excited about what's getting ready to happen for you. The trouble that I see a lot of people have is that they choose too many big rocks. As a rule of thumb, I never choose more than three.

> "If it's not on your calendar, it doesn't exist."
> —Paul Orberson

Should Do

Should Do items also come from your Activity Tracker. They will eventually move to the *Must Do* list, but for now they take second priority when scheduling. If time permits, these things will get on your schedule, but only after you have scheduled time for your *Must Do's*. I would encourage you to work from ahead instead of from behind. You see, most people are always working from behind; this causes unnecessary stress and can be avoided with proper PREPARATION. That's how I worked my network marketing business in the beginning, which created the strain we talked about earlier in this chapter. I had not learned how to PREPARE to win yet.

Could Do

Could Do items are those tasks that we should delegate out to others or know that they may not get done at all. *Could Do* items are very dangerous. These things masquerade as *Must Do* or *Should Do* items, but they don't move us closer to our goals. Cleaning out the junk drawer in your kitchen is a *Could Do* item. Sure it needs to be done... but someone else can do it or it can just wait. In network marketing, I see folks all the time that are extremely busy doing "the business." They have great intentions, but their actions bring no production because they are focused on *Could Do* tasks. They are organizing their organizer or spending hours designing the perfect flyer for their upcoming event. Don't let that be you. Know the difference in *Must Do, Should Do*, and *Could Do* items and delegate your time to them appropriately.

Below is an example of a portion of my Weekly To Do List; yours will be specific to your goals and your priorities.

WEEKLY TO DO LIST...

MUST DO!	SHOULD DO!	COULD DO!
FAITH		
MATTHEW 18 JOHN 7-8		
JOHN 9-10 LUKE 10-11		
LUKE 12-13 LUKE 14-15		
LUKE 16-17		
FINANCE		
SUE SMITH LINDA TAYLOR		FLYER FOR EVENT
CHRIS THOMPSON BOB WHITE		
JOHN DOE		

It's Show Time!

Now, let's take the bull by the horns and stop telling people where we will be in the future and what we will accomplish in the next one, three, and five years, and instead start showing them. You *show* by committing your goals to paper and following through with actions. Having a written plan for your life is the best way to organize your thoughts, select your priorities, maximize the use of your time, and hold yourself accountable.

3. Decide When to Take the Small Bite

In the second step of creating an Action Plan for reaching your goals, I coached you on how to measure your progress and keep track of whether you do or do not take that smallest bite (daily, weekly, or monthly action). In the third step we will decide specifically when we are going to take that smallest bite (daily, weekly, or monthly action). The final tool that we will use to plan our life and business is the one I call the Daily Time Budget.

C. Daily Time Budget

the
🍎 **A.P.P.L.E.**
Chris D. Estes *Principle*

DAILY TIME BUDGET

Must Do List	Should Do List	Could Do List

5:30 AM	2:30 PM	
6:00 AM	3:00 PM	
6:30 AM	3:30 PM	
7:00 AM	4:00 PM	
7:30 AM	4:30 PM	
8:00 AM	5:00 PM	
8:30 AM	5:30 PM	
9:00 AM	6:00 PM	
9:30 AM	6:30 PM	
10:00 AM	7:00 PM	
10:30 AM	7:30 PM	
11:00 AM	8:00 PM	
11:30 AM	8:30 PM	
NOON	9:00 PM	
12:30 PM	9:30 PM	
1:00 PM	10:00 PM	
1:30 PM	10:30 PM	
2:00 PM	11:00 PM	

FACT!

Once I have the daily activities for each of my Buckets listed on the Weekly Activity Tracker and have prioritized into *Must Do's*, *Should Do's*, and *Could Do's* on the Weekly To Do list, I then allocate my time appropriately on the Daily Time Budget.

If you created just one Bucket to start, I would recommend that you work backward to get the actions you want listed on your Weekly Activity Tracker and monitor this for a month. Then, proceed with the process once you feel comfortable by adding the additional tools such as the Weekly To Do List and Daily Time Budget. If you dove in and created several Buckets, I recommend following through with all activities for each Bucket, until you complete the Daily Time Budget. Your progress will amaze you.

> Prioritize *Must Do's, Should Do's, and Could Do's.*

Working from my *Touch 5* example, the Daily Time Budget is where I write the names and phone numbers of the five people that I will be calling that day into the time slot when I will be calling them. This is a big rock for me, so once those names hit my schedule it's a fact that they are getting a call. If your big rock is to *Prospect 3* new people for your business, then the same rules apply. Write their names and phone numbers into a time slot.

One of the goals I have in my FITNESS Bucket is to get up at 6:00 a.m. everyday. I do this for several reasons, but the biggest is that it allows me two hours of productive time before the rest of the world gets up and going: two hours that I can have everyday without outside distractions. From 6:00 a.m. to 8:00 a.m. I am in fully-focused mode. I call this time block my *Start Strong* time.

Having a *Start Strong* routine is very important. I get a thrill from productivity, and nothing feels better to me than knowing that by 8:00 a.m. I have already accomplished a majority of the items that are listed on my Activity Tracker. *Start Strong* time sets the tone for the rest of the day. The key to anyone's *Start Strong* routine is to ask this question, "What am I doing?"

Everyone's *Start Strong* routine will be unique to them because we all have different goals on our Life Plan. But, just to give you an example, let me walk you through mine. You can adopt what you like and add your own flavor to create your own *Start Strong* routine.

I am by no means what you would consider a morning person, so I have to set my alarm for 5:45 a.m. It just feels nice to get to hit the snooze button a time or two. By 6:00 a.m. I'm up and out of bed. In the beginning I tried doing part of my *Start Strong* routine from bed, but it was too tempting to doze back off. So now I make myself get up. And, like I mentioned in the chapter on attitude, this occasionally requires me to talk a bit of smack to myself. But, whatever works for you is fine by me.

The network marketing company I'm affiliated with is a nutritional company with great products, so the first thing I do once I'm out of bed is fuel my body with some great nutrition while speaking seeds of increase into my life with my personal commercial. I close out the first hour of my *Start Strong* routine with the following:

- Daily Bible reading using the outline from www.bibleyear.com
- Devotional
- Review my Life Plan goals and planning tools (Answering the question *"What am I doing?"*)

- Read ten pages of a personal development book

From 7:00 a.m. to 8:00 a.m. I work on the most important project of the day, one of my big rocks. I use this time to focus, without distractions, on the one thing that will move me closest to my goal that day, that month, that quarter, or that year. This project comes from my Weekly To Do list's *Must Do* section.

I will pause for a moment here because I know that you may be thinking, "Chris, I have a full-time job, I have to get ready and get the kids to school on time. There's no way I can take two hours to *Start Strong*. This works great for you, but it is not practical for me."

WRONG!

Sure you can *Start Strong*. You may not be able to start with a two-hour time block, but you can start with 30 minutes and let it grow over time. Heck, make it 15 minutes and let *that* grow over time. The key is that you START by asking yourself, "What am I doing?" The answer is always found when you review your Life Plan, your Weekly Activity Tracker, your Weekly To Do List, and your Daily Time Budget.

DAILY TIME BUDGET

Must Do List	Should Do List	Could Do List
TOUCH 5:		DELEGATE TO BETTY:
SUE SMITH		FLYER FOR EVENT
LINDA TAYLOR		
CHRIS THOMPSON		
BOB WHITE		
JOHN DOE		

5:30 AM		2:30 PM	
6:00 AM	START STRONG	3:00 PM	
6:30 AM	↓ BIBLE: MATTHEW 18	3:30 PM	
7:00 AM	↓ WRITE BOOK: INTRO	4:00 PM	
7:30 AM	↓	4:30 PM	
8:00 AM		5:00 PM	
8:30 AM		5:30 PM	
9:00 AM		6:00 PM	
9:30 AM		6:30 PM	
10:00 AM	LINDA TAYLOR 317-4567 JOHN DOE 645-6789	7:00 PM	
10:30 AM	BOB WHITE 402-1234 SUE SMITH 987-2345	7:30 PM	
11:00 AM	CHRIS THOMPSON 768-7373	8:00 PM	
11:30 AM		8:30 PM	
NOON		9:00 PM	

Life Plan

BUCKET	GOAL (1 YEAR)	DEADLINE	ACTION PLAN	HOW MEASURED	WHEN DONE
FAITH	READ ENTIRE BIBLE	12/31	DAILY READING FOLLOWING OUTLINE FROM WWW.BIBLEYEAR.COM	ACTIVITY TRACKER	START STRONG
FAMILY	12 MADDIE/DADDY DATES	12/31	SCHEDULE DATE DAYS 3 MONTHS IN ADVANCE, LOCK IN ON MY CALENDAR	RECORD DATES COMPLETED ON LIFE PLAN	SCHEDULED AT EACH CALIBRATION
FINANCE	CONNECT WITH 1300 PEOPLE	12/31	TOUCH 5 PROGRAM	ACTIVITY TRACKER	BIG ROCK TIME BLOCK

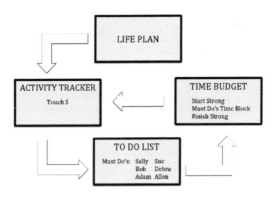

It's Game Time!

I remember from my coaching days just how much my players hated to do drills. They would complain about how it was a waste of their time. Some would just go through the motions, getting it done but not actually focusing on the details of the drill because they didn't see the value. You may be feeling the same way about the PREPARATION steps just explained throughout this chapter: it feels like pointless drills to you. But I want to encourage you — just like I encouraged my players — don't just go through the motions. Going through the motions will be a waste of your time. Focusing while you PREPARE is the total opposite of time wasted, it is the best investment you will ever have of your time. Just as drills in sports train players to respond properly during game time, PREPARATION in life and your network marketing business will train you to respond appropriately when distractions come and life tries to throw you off course.

It is game time. You could just wing it and see how the ball bounces, or you could PREPARE and start each day knowing that your game is already won. Which sounds better for you?

Prepare points to remember...

- The power of preparation.

- Have a Life Plan.

- What's your definition of success?

    o STEP 1- Identify your Buckets and your WHY.

    o STEP 2- Commit your goals to paper and set deadlines.

    o STEP 3- Create an Action Plan.

    o Work backward.

    o Measure your progress.

        ▪ Weekly Activity Tracker

        ▪ Weekly To Do List.

    o Decide when to take the small bite.

        ▪ Daily Time Budget

3

a.p.P.l.e.

"P" stands for PERFORM

*"Ideas are a dime a dozen.
People who implement them are priceless."
- Mary Kay Ash*

Take Action

While presenting for various network marketing teams, I often start the presentation by testing the level of initiative in the audience. I'll stand on stage and hold up a $20 bill and lead with a question:

"Who wants this?"

Most people raise their hands, and some even shout out, "I do!" But there have been only a handful of occasions when someone actually came up and took the money from me right after I asked. Nine times out of ten, I just stand there waiting until someone finally rushes up to the stage and snatches the money from my hand.

The point of this illustration is simple. Ideas, plans, and preparation only have value when they are acted upon. You see, merely wanting the $20 bill didn't make them any richer.

We all want to have more, be more, and do more, but in order to see the results of our desires we have to PERFORM by taking action. I have found that there are three types of people in the network marketing profession, and in life, when it comes to PERFORMING:

Those who MAKE things happen!

I would recommend you choose to be this type. These people take action and make corrections as they go.

Those who WATCH things happen!

These people are usually in the right place at the right time; they just don't ever take advantage of opportunities because of some limiting belief they have.

Those who WONDER, what just happened?

These people live in left field; things tend to happen *to* them, never *for* them.

Getting Ready To...

To succeed, we should jump as quickly at opportunities as we do to conclusions. You see, it's the start that stops most people. The majority of people spend their whole lives *getting ready to...* They tell themselves, and the people around them, that they're *getting ready to* start their own business, they're *getting ready to* talk to people, they're *getting ready to* write a book, they're *getting ready to* PERFORM by taking action on their hopes and dreams. I have to tell you, the greatest time wasted is the time getting started. Remember, desire is not enough, good intentions are not enough, and talk is not enough. Success requires you to PERFORM, so go ahead and start now by simply taking a bite out of your A.P.P.L.E and PERFORM today. Tomorrow, next week, later, sometime, and someday are just synonyms for the word NEVER. Stop wasting time *getting ready to,* and take action now. Remember, *one of these days* means none of these days.

Give Me a Break!

I often tell this story that I read in Jack Canfield's book, *The Success Principles*, when training on taking action:

> *A man goes to church and prays, "God, I need a break. I need to win the state lottery. I am counting on you, God." Having not won the lottery, the man returns to church a week later and once again prays, "God, about that state lottery... I have been kind to my wife. I have given up drinking. I have been really good. Give me a break. Let me win the lottery." A week later, still no richer, he returns to pray once again. "God, I don't seem to be getting through to you on this state lottery thing. I have been using positive self-talk, saying affirmations, and visualizing the money. Give me a break, God. Let me win the lottery."*
>
> *Suddenly the heavens open up, white lights and heavenly music flood into the church, and a deep voice says, "My son, give me a break! Buy a lottery ticket!"[1]*

Take Bite #3

The third bite of the A.P.P.L.E. that I eat everyday stands for the word PERFORM. Just like the man in this story, most people wish, hope, and even pray that that their circumstances will change. But as Paul Orberson told me, "God feeds the birds every morning, but he doesn't throw the worms down their throats." It's up to each of us to PERFORM the tasks, day by day and bite by bite that will produce the results that we are preparing for.

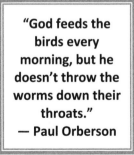

"God feeds the birds every morning, but he doesn't throw the worms down their throats."
— Paul Orberson

Why some WILL and some WON'T...

In the beginning... Why some WILL PERFORM and some WON'T!

Analysis Paralysis

On the front end of any new endeavor, some people won't PERFORM because they get what I call *Analysis Paralysis*, which sets in when people think that they have to know every tiny little detail there is to know about the task before they can take any action. These people are afraid to start because there is a chance that they will encounter a situation that they won't already know how to solve. Or they are afraid that they'll get asked a question that they don't already know the answer to. If this is your mindset, we must change it quickly. I can guarantee you that had I waited until I knew everything about starting a business, everything about network marketing, and everything about the product that my company has, I would not be where I am today. I would instead still be teaching and coaching, raising other people's kids and never seeing my own.

Find a Way!

When I first started my network marketing business, I quickly adopted the "earn while you learn" mentality. I didn't do this because I was wise beyond my years; I did this because when I first started, like I said in the chapter on attitude, I was working out of desperation... not inspiration. I didn't have time to wait. I was broke and had a baby on the way, and that baby wasn't waiting. *(She actually decided to arrive a month early.)* So I found a way to get started with no money by using a card called "Master." I found a way to earn my investment back before the credit card bill came due by sharing the products and opportunity with everyone I came in contact with. And I found a way to learn the business of network marketing as I was doing the business of network marketing. I learned by doing, by getting some things right and getting some things wrong.

Experience is the best teacher.

There was a man in my town that started the business when I did, but he hasn't seen the same results that I have. The difference between his success and mine lies in *Analysis Paralysis*. He spent his first two years trying to figure out the compensation plan before taking action, while I went to work. I still don't really understand the compensation plan; all I know is the more people you help, the more money you make. I have found throughout my life that experience is the best teacher. Webster's Dictionary has three definitions for the word *experience*: all three definitions include the word *DO*. That, my friend, is what we call a clue. Don't let *Analysis Paralysis* steal the future that you desire and deserve. DO the things that will lead you to your goals even when you are afraid of them, DO the things even when you don't feel like it, DO the things even when they aren't easy, and keep DOING the things until they are done.

> **Don't let *Analysis Paralysis* steal the future that you desire and deserve.**

How to overcome *Analysis Paralysis*:

Expect the unexpected!

A great way to ease the anxiety that comes with stepping out of your comfort zone is to resolve up front that unexpected things are going to arise. Prepare yourself by expecting to encounter situations that you won't know the answer to. Be aware from the start that it is highly unlikely that everything is going to go as you initially plan for it to. If you expect the unexpected, then you maintain control. You have a mindset that will allow you to respond to these situations instead of react. Here is what I mean by that:

Respond - a reply to an issue that creates a solution.

React - a reply to an issue that creates additional issues.

Pop Quiz!

Big exams in school were easy to prepare for; the dates were on the syllabus that you got the first day of class, so you had plenty of time to study. But on occasion, the teachers would hit you with what they call a pop quiz. Pop quizzes are designed to catch you off guard; they are designed to make sure you've been paying attention in class and doing the small assignments each day that would build into the larger concepts needed for the scheduled exam. Pop quizzes are tests designed to see if you have been consistent with eating your A.P.P.L.E.

If you are expecting the unexpected, when unexpected situations happen you can laugh and say, "I've been expecting a pop quiz." And since you HAVE been eating your A.P.P.L.E. everyday, you are well equipped to *respond* and not *react*.

In life and in the business of network marketing, pop quizzes happen on a regular basis. I gave the example earlier of the pop quiz that my top leaders and I faced on our trip to Bora Bora. Another pop quiz that any network marketer should expect is for a lot of their people to quit. I like to tell all new folks in the business that it's easier to give birth than to raise the dead. Remember, you never lose anyone in your business, or in life, that you shouldn't lose. When the world says, "No!" you say, "Next!" So get your hopes up, knowing that your best days are just one more "No!" away!

> **When the world says, "No!" you say, "Next!"**

80

Involve others!

A majority of people will follow through on a commitment that they have made to someone else, long before they will follow through on one that they have made to themselves. If you are one of those folks, then set yourself up for success by involving others in your plan. Tell people you respect about what you are doing; ask them to join in, or at least check in with you on your progress. Put pressure on yourself to PERFORM by including an accountability partner, someone whom you would hate to disappoint.

Accountability Partners

I have a different accountability partner for each of my Buckets. These are people whom I've elected to monitor the progress I'm making toward reaching my goals. These people know what daily actions I should be taking, and they call my hand when I don't follow through. When choosing an accountability partner for yourself, keep in mind it must be someone strong enough to point out your shortcomings and someone you respect too much to disappoint. Set a time each week to report your PERFORMANCE to your accountability partner. These calls are game changing; it's never fun to miss your mark when you know people are watching you.

Create a Habit of getting out of your *Safe Zone*!

Eleanor Roosevelt is quoted as saying, "Do one thing every day that scares you." In general, we are programmed from a very early age to spend a lot of time trying to avoid discomfort or scary situations. Even 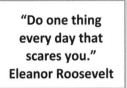 the thought of these situations can paralyze us. However, by avoiding the uncomfortable or scary situations, we are restricting ourselves to a small zone of comfort, our *safe zone...* and do you know how many exciting moments take place inside the safe zone?

NOT MANY!

But if we can train ourselves to step outside our safe zone at least once every day, soon it will seem less scary. And soon we will unfold a whole new world of possibilities. Remember, according to Brian Klemmer in his book *The Compassionate Samurai*, "Courage isn't the absence of fear, it's acting in the face of it. It's being afraid of something and doing it anyway."[2]

> **"Courage isn't the absence of fear, it's acting in the face of it."**
> **—Brian Klemmer**

I read a story once about how Warren Buffett, a billionaire investor, was afraid of public speaking. He said that his knees knocked so bad that he could hardly maintain focus. Buffett enrolled in a Dale Carnegie course, and when asked about his reasoning he replied, "I didn't take the course so my knees would stop knocking; I took the course so that I could speak while my knees knocked."

Once they do get started... Why some WILL PERFORM and some WON'T!

It's not Magic, it's Monotony...

I do a lot of consulting with other distributors in the network marketing profession. They are all eager to know what "the secret" is... what the "magical thing" is that I did to achieve the results that I now have. They say things like, "I'd love to do what you do." My response to them is always the same, "You can do what I do, if you are willing to do what I've done." I go on to explain to them that the actions I took to get to this point in my career are not magical and they're not a secret. They are actually simple. And therein lies the problem, it's not magic; it's monotony.

"So Chris, what did you do in the beginning?" they will ask, "The same thing I do now." I always say, "Listen and talk to people every day." There are really only three rules to a successful network marketing business, and they apply to most other businesses:

1. Talk to people.

2. Talk to more people.

3. Talk to many more people.

Vomit Comets!

By "talking", I primarily mean listening and building a relationship. Most people in the network marketing profession become what I call *vomit comets*. They throw up the information all over their prospects or potential business partners. That's not good. Too much information given all at once makes people think you are trying to sell them something. People don't like to be sold; they like to buy.

There's an old saying: "A person convinced against their will is of the same opinion still." Massive success is never achieved alone. When talking to people, excitement is the name of the game. Excitement is contagious. Excitement is caught... not taught. Get excited, listen to people, and make a connection. After all, another old saying says, "To sell John Brown what John Brown buys, you have to see things

"A person convinced against their will is of the same opinion still."
—Unknown

through John Brown's eyes." If you want people to join you, they must feel connected to you.

Like the three rules for success mentioned earlier, my Action Plan in my business is very repetitive. I act on what I like to call the *FUNdamental 5*... and I do it everyday.

The FUNdamental 5 of PERFORMING in Network Marketing!

I first came up with the *FUNdamental 5* concept after a meeting with John Maxwell where he explained to me his *Rule of 5*. Maxwell's *Rule of 5* states that no matter your endeavor, you can simplify the action plan down to five specific tasks that need to be done everyday to achieve your goals. Those five things will be different for everyone because they are specific to the goal. To illustrate his point he relates reaching our goal to chopping down a tree. If we want to cut down a tree (the goal) and we have an axe (an action plan), we should simply take five swings (the daily actions) each day, and the tree will fall. The tree will fall with what seems like little effort because we've been disciplined and diligent in taking just five swings each day. Below we will go through the *Rule of 5*, or as I call it the *FUNdamental 5*, that I created for PERFORMING in network marketing.

1. Prospect List

In network marketing, this is where you should always start. Make a list; write down the names of everyone you know. Who could benefit from the product or service you have to offer? Who could benefit from the business opportunity you have to offer? You must review and revise this list every day. No one ever comes off of this list; it only grows. In fact, I often tell the team when I train that the only way people come off the list is:

They join the business or they pass away.

Recently, I was on the phone with a new distributor. I told him to make a list of people who had complained about time, money, and health issues and also people he would love to partner with in business. I then said that I would call him back in 15 minutes to review the list with him. It wasn't two minutes after that call that my daughter, Maddie, walked out of her room and said, "Daddy, I have my list. I have Max, Ava, Malia, and Kayla." Of course her paper was filled with scribbles because she's only four years old, but my point is this: Who can make a list? ANYBODY.

2. Pique

We have two ears and only one mouth for a reason: to listen more than we talk. Listen to the people around you, including those who are on your list. Ask them questions and then listen again. Keep it very simple; if you are a good listener everyone will tell you what it is they are looking for, what it is that they need. John Maxwell always says, "People don't care how much you know until they know how much you care."[3] The goal is not to sell them on something; the goal is to provide a possible solution. The goal is to create curiosity by piquing their interest.

Who Can Pique?

To refer to my daughter again, one day she rode with me to the local fitness center. I dropped her off at the daycare there while I went to swim laps. I was booked to speak in Canada the next day for some network marketing events, and Maddie gets excited when I travel because I always come back with a surprise for her. Her excitement bubbled over as she told the two daycare workers that her daddy was going to Canada. They asked, "What does your daddy do?" and Maddie replied, *"He shows people how..."* (What a great four-word phrase!)

"He shows people how to make money."

With that, she piqued their interest. When I arrived to pick her up, the two ladies asked me what I did for a living that was taking me to Canada. *Are you kidding me?* Who can pique interest? ANYBODY. Who got the commission check on that enrollment? My daughter, and she's four years old.

3. Pass

The pass is my favorite *P*. Once your prospect is curious and has a ton of questions, your only job is to get out of the way by passing them to a tool or a resource. You are not a *TOOL*. Typically passing prospects to a video is best because it provides a visual and is not time consuming.

Who Can Pass?

After the ladies from the fitness center daycare asked me what I did, I responded the way I always do, with two four-word phrases and a conjunction between. *"I'm glad you asked, BUT I don't have time."* I share this with you because that day I collected their contact information and immediately PASSED them a video to review. How hard was that? NOT VERY. Who can do that? ANYBODY.

4. Plug

Once the prospect has taken a look at the information they have been passed to, plug them immediately into a business partner who can relate to their want, need, or situation. This person will share their story and answer the prospect's questions.

Who Can Plug?

After the two ladies had reviewed the video, I followed up with a call and asked them what they liked and what they wanted to learn more about. After listening to their wants and concerns, I plugged them into a person of commonality; in this case another female who'd achieved success in the area where they were interested in achieving success. Do you think there was a connection? Of course. Would it have been as effective if I had tried to do it myself? Nope. Why? Because for starters I'm a guy. And second, plugging someone else in teaches duplication. Remember, it's not what works in this business; it's what duplicates.

5. Promote and Present

What to Promote:

Events. J Paul Getty said, "I'd rather have one percent of one hundred people's efforts than 100% of my own." Being intentional in promoting your existing team and potential prospects to events is essential for the growth of your business. Consistency is key. Everyday I promote my people to the next event. A presentation is just an overview of all you have to offer. Presentations come in many different forms, such as conference calls, home events, webinars, and Super Saturdays.

People. I've already mentioned my program called *Touch 5* in which I call five new people in my organization everyday to endorse them, to encourage them, and to offer support to foster their business growth. How hard is that to do? NOT VERY.

Where to Present:

At any event listed above.

Who Can Promote And Present?

The two daycare workers from the fitness center had busy evening schedules; therefore I promoted them to a conference call so they could listen to more information while at home. After taking them through this process, they did decide to get started with the company.

It's simple, but not easy.

None of the components of the *FUNdamental 5* are difficult to do, but most people won't do them. They would rather nod their head and say, "Okay Chris, but what else?" Everyone always wants a different answer, but what I described is what I did and still do... and not just one day here or there, but everyday. It's called eating your A.P.P.L.E, and this is done for network marketers by PERFORMING with the *FUNdamental 5* of this business.

It's so simple, but it's not easy, and that's why most people won't do it. They want something like a magic pill they can take and automatically lose thirty pounds without having to change their eating habits or heaven forbid, exercise. They want it to be a bean that they can plant and grow a money tree overnight. They want instant gratification without having to make any changes that require too much effort or willpower. But you are smarter than that, aren't you? You know that dedication, consistency, and commitment to *The A.P.P.L.E. Principle* are what lead to massive success. You are unique because you know that success is a process, success takes time, and success requires you to PERFORM.

After some success... Why some will continue to PERFORM and some won't.

They Lose Focus...

So far in this book we have learned how to choose and maintain a positive attitude and how to determine what we want in life and business, and how to make a plan to get it. Next, it's time for the rubber to meet the road. It's time to PERFORM. You have prepared properly so the road is straight and it leads directly to your goals and dreams. In fact, you should have a clear vision of exactly how to get to your destination. You are PERFORMING and having some success; all you have to do now is keep driving until you reach your destination. Unfortunately, this is easier said than done because all along the roadside are *distractions*.

These *distractions* also have a job; it's to test you, to see if the things you said you wanted to achieve *really* are what you want. The *distractions* are allowed to do anything they want to tempt you to pull off the road. They offer instant fame, power, success in another area, recognition, and easy money. The only thing the *distractions* can't do is get on the road and stop you. This means that leaving the road (the road that is clearly marked and headed straight to your goal) will always be your choice.

The facts are that laser focus does not come naturally, and it does not come easily. This is especially true in today's world where all boundaries between work and personal life have been eliminated. These days, it's easy to become distracted and preoccupied with mindless, nonproductive tasks that subtly tempt us to leave the road.

> **Distractions test you, to see if the things you said you wanted to achieve really are what you want.**

Dealing with Distractions.

How can we maintain focus when we are constantly being pulled in a million different directions? We must choose the main things, the big rocks from the story in the chapter on preparation. The big rocks are the specific tasks that we must do every day to keep us in forward momentum down the road toward success. We must never confuse movement for achievement or activity for productivity. These things are distinctly different, and confusing them can be detrimental. Assign time on your schedule for specific productive activities, and then guard that time with your life.

There are several time thieves out there that will do all they can to knock you off course. There's no better way to destroy hopes, dreams, and ambitions than by allowing outside influences to steal your time. But unfortunately, most people allow this to happen without even realizing it. These *time thieves* come in several forms. There are plenty of modern ways for us to lose time, such as Tweeting, Pinning, Instagramming, and Facebooking... but the oldest and most reliable *time thieves* are the TV and telephone.

Time Thieves

It still happens to me on occasion with the telephone. I sit down during the time that I have blocked off to PERFORM a big rock task, and just as I'm in the groove and making progress... RING, RING, RING. Even more tempting for me is the DING that happens when I have a text message. "Don't answer it, Chris, it can wait," my head says, but curiosity gets the best of me as I wonder, "Whose number is that? What do they want? Maybe it's an emergency..." WRONG! It's not an emergency; it's a time thief, and they didn't even have to break in to steal my time. I opened the door and welcomed them in with open arms and a nice cold drink. Before I know it twenty minutes have passed, I've lost all momentum on the big rock task I was supposed to be working on, and now I'm officially behind for the rest of the day.

For the longest time in my network marketing business I was "Rep Services Kentucky". If you had a problem, you could just give me a call or shoot me a text and I'd spend all day trying to get it worked out. Those distractions almost killed my business and me. How often do you allow your time to be stolen away by outside influences? Block off your time and then guard it with your life.

The Key to Consistent High Performance...

Stay Hungry!

The period after a success, after a win, can become a dangerous time. I remember when I hit my first big goal... the first big rank in my business. It happened about eight months after I started. This rank basically meant that I was now making more than double in my part-time business what I was at my full-time job of teaching and coaching. I was ecstatic; it felt like I had just won the Tour de France or something. I could breathe easier now, knowing that my financial situation was turning around. I thought I had arrived, *again*. I'd hit the goal I had set out to achieve. So I flipped into maintenance mode with my chest puffed out, and I took my achievement and bragged about it to Paul Orberson. He congratulated me and then asked what I wanted to achieve next. "Well, I hadn't really thought about it," I said. Then he said something that I will never forget, "Chris, if what you did yesterday still looks big to you, you haven't done much today."

OUCH!

Sometimes we feel tempted toward complacency, especially if we lack another bigger goal. We can become satisfied and let down our guard. Momentum leaks. This is why we must always have our goals growing as we do. We should be shooting at a moving target, a target that is consistently out ahead of us.

When you think you have arrived, think again. Paul went on to tell me, "It is important to celebrate our success, but not camp out there. Nothing keeps you broke longer than yesterday's success."

How to ward off a complacency mindset:

- Understand that true success is a journey, not a destination.
- Strive for continual growth. You are either moving forward or you are moving backward. There is no such thing as remaining the same.
- Set bigger goals, ones that force you to stretch. Playing it small does the world no good.

Do It... TODAY, TOMORROW, and the NEXT Day!

You can't build your future or your legacy on what you are *going to do*. Our future is determined by what we actually do TODAY. When's the best time to plant an oak tree? Thirty years ago. When is the next best time? TODAY. So, don't put off until tomorrow what you can get done today. Go out and get whatever it is that you desire, go get all of the things that you deserve. PERFORM the actions no matter how insignificant they may seem, no matter how mundane it may be, and do them consistently until you reach your goals. Take the third bite out of your A.P.P.L.E. everyday, and PERFORM.

Perform Points to remember...

- Why some WILL and some WON'T.
  - In the beginning...
    - *Analysis Paralysis*
  - Once they do get started...
    - It's not magic, it's monotony
    - The *FUNdamental 5*
  - After some success...
    - They lose focus
    - Dealing with distractions
  - The key to consistent high performance.
    - Stay Hungry

4

a.p.p.L.e.

"L" stands for LEARN

"The most successful people in life are the ones who ask questions. They're always learning. They're always growing. They're always pushing."
- Robert Kiyosaki

After You Know It All...

It is safe to say that my philosophy concerning self-education, personal development, and continual LEARNING has done a complete 180 since the summer of 2008. Like I said before, when I was teaching and coaching, I read what was required of me to do my job, but nothing extra. I saw no value in LEARNING any more than I already knew. After all, I knew it all, I thought, and therefore had no plan to better myself. This changed, however, when a friend and mentor of mine asked me over lunch one day what I was currently reading. I dodged the question as much as I could because I wasn't reading anything. In fact, I hadn't read an entire book since college, and even then it was just to impress a girl, not to LEARN anything.

My friend went on to quote John Wooden, who said, "It's what you LEARN after you know it all that counts." What you

LEARN after you know it all is what separates those who attain short-term success from those who achieve lasting results. You see, short-term success can be obtained through hard work... but to achieve lasting results you must be continually growing better and bigger.

BETTER than you were yesterday.

BIGGER than any issue that will arise.

Since that conversation I have made continual LEARNING and personal growth not only a goal of mine, but also the biggest goal I have. In each Bucket of my life there is a goal for growth and continual LEARNING. I understand that I'm not going to get better or bigger by accident, so I have a plan. These days my personal development routine is simple; I listen a little and read a little every day. My car doesn't leave my driveway unless there is a personal development CD playing.

> **I understand that I'm not going to get better or bigger by accident, so I have a plan.**

It wasn't a difficult change to make. It's still not hard to do; you just have to start doing it. When it comes to reading, don't be misled — I'm not a bookworm. The first year I started my growth plan with a goal of reading five pages of an uplifting book first thing in the morning. Then, at night before bed, I'd do it again. How long does it take to read five pages? NOT VERY. It's easy to do and easy not to do. It's a choice, one that over time can make a HUGE difference. For me, I simply focused on LEARNING a little every day; ten total pages. Not much, right? But, over the course of thirty days, that's 300 pages.

Think about it: 300 pages is typically more than one book. What if you read one book a month and applied just one concept from that book into your business and into your life? That's twelve new concepts a year. Do you think that would make a positive difference in your life and your business? ABSOLUTELY. It made such an impact on my life that I now have my goal set at ten pages in the morning and ten at night. Page by page and bite by bite I am altering the course of my life, and it all started by adopting the principle of an A.P.P.L.E. a day.

It wasn't a huge change, but it made a huge difference in multiple areas of my life, especially in my finances. I guess what Jim Rohn said is true: a formal education will make you a living (I had a bachelors degree, a masters degree, and a pile of debt), but self-education will make you a fortune. That's why I believe 100% in the power of network marketing and the opportunity for growing people. I would not be where I am today, having time freedom, choices, and options, had I not started network marketing and bought into the concept of personal development and continual growth.

Take Bite #4

The fourth bite of the A.P.P.L.E. that I eat every day stands for the word LEARN. Like I said, every morning when I wake up the biggest goal that I have is to do my very best *that day*, to be my very best *that day*, and to grow as much as possible *that day*. It's my belief that when you set personal growth as a top priority for each day, life gets very exciting because personal growth creates limitless possibilities. We should all be excited knowing that we can have more and do more simply because we can become more. Looking back, I can clearly see that any success I have achieved and any money that I have made has just been a byproduct of continual personal development and growth.

I love what Jim Rohn said about this subject: "Every life form seems to strive to its maximum except human beings. How tall will a tree grow? As tall as it possibly can.

> "Every life form seems to strive to its maximum except human beings."
> —Jim Rohn

97

Human beings, on the other hand, have been given the dignity of choice. You can choose to be all or you can choose to be less."

I can think of a few reasons why we might sometimes choose to grow less than we possibly can.

Growing is a struggle.

You will face problems such as ridicule and rejection. But I've learned that the secret to success, not only in network marketing but also in life, is not to get rid of, avoid, or shrink from your problems. The secret is to grow yourself so that you're bigger than any problem. I don't just go through the storms, I GROW through them, and I would encourage you to do the same.

The results of the growth don't come as quickly as we would like.

In a society that thrives on instant gratification, true and lasting success can be hard to wait for. Warren Buffet said, "Someone is sitting in the shade today because someone planted a tree a long time ago." We have to acknowledge the concept of invisible results. Just as it's the root that creates the fruit, the invisible is what creates the visible in due time.

We reached a goal, and now we think we have arrived!

This truth has been evident in my own life, and I see it all the time in people who are new to the business of network marketing. When I meet with my mentoring group, *The Nest*, we always talk about how to stay hungry. Sometimes the biggest obstacle for them in getting to $20,000 a month is the $10,000 a month they are already making. I know that *UP* is not an easy direction — it defies gravity. But *UP* is not impossible if you have a focus on continual growth.

Growth is hard; developing your talent is hard. Progress requires you to get out of your comfort zone and stretch, and sometimes stretching doesn't feel good. We must realize, however, that growth stops when we lose the tension between where we are and where we could be. We all have to continue to stretch, even when it's uncomfortable. You see, rubber bands may come in different shapes and colors, but they all work on the same principle: they must be stretched to be effective.

To be successful and effective, we must learn to stretch to the challenges of life. Most people stretch a little and rest a lot; this gives them a vacation mentality or a retirement mindset. From 2001 to 2008, that's where I was, mentally retired. I had stopped stretching and

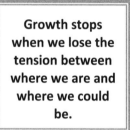

> **Growth stops when we lose the tension between where we are and where we could be.**

therefore had stopped growing. Please realize that when you stop stretching you become boring. Nothing is more boring than a person who has not had a new thought in the last year. Think about me... I hadn't had a new thought in eight years, really. Don't be that person. Choose to grow as tall as you possibly can and stretch as much as you possibly can.

Your Gift Makes Room For You.

One thing that people often assume is that abundance is only for the few, the lucky ones, the ones who were born with talents that not everyone has. Listen, this is simply not the case. There are seeds of greatness in all of us, things that we can do better than anyone else, and these are our gifts. In the book of Proverbs it says that a man's gift makes room for him and brings him before great men. This should excite us to know that everyone has a special gift and that gift is what will open the door of opportunities for us to reach our full potential, to have an abundant life. Here, though, is the kicker: that gift only makes room for us... it won't keep us there. In order to actually achieve results we have to grow and develop our gift, and this is where the majority of folks get left behind. Growth requires intentionality.

Be A Habitual Learner!

Through my experiences over the past several years I have become very conscious about maintaining consistent growth. After all, according to John Maxwell, "If you want to become a continual winner, you must be a habitual learner."[1] So, be intentional about LEARNING and personal growth. To do this you must ask yourself the following five questions:

1. What am I feeding my mind?
2. Who am I hanging around?
3. What environment am I choosing to live in?
4. Am I seeking advice from credible mentors?
5. Am I being a good example for others to model themselves after?

These were game-changing questions for my life and business. In fact, these are questions I ask myself at the end of every day, every week, and every month. These are questions I would encourage you to begin asking yourself as well.

Game-Changing Questions:

1. What am I feeding my mind?

Before 2008...

Before 2008, my reading consisted of magazines such as *Runners World, Triathlete, People,* and anything published about Kentucky Basketball. Now, I'm not saying those things are bad or that there isn't a time for them; it's just that none of those publications was moving me toward anything. Heck, like I said, before the summer of 2008, I hadn't read an actual book since college, and even then I just did it to impress a girl. I know, wrong reason. But, I've since LEARNED that if you want things on the higher shelf in life — dream home, nice cars, frequent vacations, the freedom, choices, options, and unlimited ability to give — you're going to have to stand on the books you read, the CD's you listen to, and the videos you watch to get them.

Before 2008, my car stereo was tuned in to whatever music was popular at the moment. My commute each morning was time lost listening to non-motivational music and even more non-motivational news. No one had ever shared with me that just by switching out one hour a day of listening to music for some personal development CD's, you could be an expert in any field in merely five years. It wasn't until I started my network marketing career that I was introduced to something called "Drive Time University." It wasn't until I popped that first Jim Rohn CD into my car that I started to fall in love with LEARNING. Before, I saw no value in reading outside what was mandatory at my job, I saw no value in motivational CD's *"What kind of dork listens to those?" I thought.* After all, I already knew everything I needed to know... WRONG!

Mind Meal Plan!

Your mind acts on what you feed it. What is on your Mind Meal Plan? Most people are like I was before I harnessed the power of personal development. They feed their minds the equivalent of fast food. Fast food for the mind is easy and doesn't require any preparation or effort. Whatever is on the radio, is what we listen to... Whatever is on the TV, is what we watch... Whatever is on the front page of the newspaper, is what we read.

> **Fast food for the mind is easy and doesn't require any preparation or effort.**

But just as the body diet makes the body, the mind diet makes the mind. The kind of mind food we consume determines our habits, attitudes, and personality. If all we ever listen to is music with foul language, pretty soon that is what will come out of our mouths. If all we ever read about is violence and poverty, pretty soon that will become the world we live in. Prolonged consumption of negative *mind meals* makes us think negatively. Remember:

Garbage In = Garbage Out

> **Prolonged consumption of negative mind meals makes us think negatively.**

On the bright side, consumption of positive and uplifting *mind meals* produces positive habits, positive attitudes, and positive results. It would be wonderful if our mind growled like our stomach does when it's hungry, but it doesn't. So I want to encourage you to overindulge. Go ahead and feed your mind all of the abundance and hope it can handle. It's not what the books cost. It's what it will cost you if you don't read the books. It's not what the audios cost. It's what it will cost you if you don't listen to the audios. And on the flip side, it isn't what the TV costs you to own; that is fairly inexpensive. It is what the TV costs you to watch — *time* — and that costs too much.

Think about this: before my philosophy on personal development changed I was watching a lot of TV, or what many people like to call the "Electronic Income Reducer." I was watching CNN or what I like to call, "Constant Negative News". And even though I was living paycheck-to-paycheck, I chose to spend my time watching others build their dreams rather than building my own. Don't let that be you. Be aware of what you are feeding your mind. Have a plan to block out all of the garbage and a plan to input things that are positive, uplifting, and accelerating to your growth.

2. Who am I hanging around?

Associations

It's been said that you are the average of the five people you associate with the most. The way you walk, talk, act, think, dress... your income, your accomplishments, even your values and philosophy, will reflect them. Make no mistake; the company we keep affects us. The reason *birds of a feather flock together* is simply that they are all going in the same direction, headed for the same destination. I encourage you to evaluate the people with whom you flock: where do they have you going, what do they have you thinking, and who are they helping you to become?

One of the toughest things you'll have to do is let go of some of your relationships and associations that are leading you away from your goals. I've learned that precious few people are intended to be in your life for very long. David Schwartz said, in *The Magic of Thinking BIG*, "Close contact with petty individuals develops petty habits in us... close contact with ambitious people gives us ambition."[2] It's a fact that having close companionship with people who have big ideas raises the level of our thinking. If we want to have more, do more, and be more, we must assess our associations. As the apostle Paul wrote in his letter to the church in Corinth, "Do not be deceived, bad company corrupts good character" (I Corinthians 15:33, NIV).

> "Close contact with petty individuals develops petty habits in us... close contact with ambitious people gives us ambition."
> —David Schwartz

A friend of mine grew up near the Atlantic Ocean, where people catch blue crabs for dinner. He told me that as they catch the crabs, they toss them into a bucket or basket. He said that if you have only one crab in the basket, you need a lid to keep it from crawling out, but if you've got two or more, you don't. That didn't make any sense to me until he explained further. He said that when there are several crabs, they will drag one another down so that none of them can get away.

I have found that there are some people who act the same way. The crabs in our lives are those people who are lazy and undisciplined, the ones who don't have great dreams, and despise those who do. They do all kinds of things to keep others from getting ahead, trying to prevent them from improving themselves or their situation. They use all kinds of devices to keep others in the basket with them.

You see, we must choose our travel companions carefully. You can't expect to reach your potential, attain your goals, or live a positive life while being closely associated with the Negative Nancys, Pessimist Petes, Sour Steves, and Debbie Downers of the world. The wisecracks at work that know nothing about nothing, making payments on everything, sitting at six clicks left of clueless, are not who you want on your "Top Five Friends" list.

You can stay out of the basket by refusing to be a crab. You may have to face opposition and live through times of insecurity, but you'll also get to experience freedom, increased potential, and satisfaction. Raise yourself up, and raise others with you. Had I not ended those relationships I would still be paycheck to paycheck, more month at the end of the money, raising everyone else's kids but never seeing my own.

At times, all of us will have people who leave our lives. They may not be bad people. It's just that the season for that relationship is over. Like I said, very few people are meant to be in your life for very long. People who want to live at their full potential have discovered that the "good" can often be the enemy of the "best." We must learn to "keep the best and prune the rest." We must learn to subtract those that hold us back. When I host *Getting Started* trainings for my network marketing company, I always encourage our new people to have "distributor funerals" early and often. It is a fact that you will never lose anyone in your business, or in your life for that matter, that you shouldn't lose.

Add Those Who Push You Onward...

Just as negative associations have negative effects on our potential, positive associations have positive effects on our potential. When I speak on this topic, I often tell the story of the man who put his mule in the Kentucky Derby. Everyone said to him, "You know, your mule isn't going to win." And he said, "Yeah, but I thought the company would do it some good." You may already be good. You may even be better than everyone else. But without positive outside input you will never be as good as you could be.

Self-evaluation is helpful, but evaluation from someone else is essential. Surround yourself with winners, people who exhibit and live in a way that's consistent with values and skills you want to acquire and develop. You see, the people in your life have an amazing power to influence your destiny. Every relationship you have is an association, and each association has either a positive or negative effect on you. In other words, people will either increase you or they will decrease you. I want to

> The people in your life have an amazing power to influence your destiny.

encourage you to associate with the people who increase you, who challenge you to be better, and who push you onward.

Upgrade Your Inner Circle!

To attract attractive people, you must be attractive. To attract powerful people, you must be powerful. To attract committed people, you must be committed. Understand though, some people don't need to upgrade their inner circle, because they aren't upgrading themselves. Instead of going to work on the people around you, go to work on yourself first. If you become, you will attract.

Don't join an easy crowd; you won't grow. Go where the expectations and the demands to perform are high. As King Solomon in all his wisdom said, "He who walks with the wise grows wise, but a companion of fools suffers harm" (Proverbs 13:20, NIV). If you want to be a top network marketer, then you need to make sure you're around people who are the level you want to be. If you want your spiritual life to grow, then you need to make sure you around people who are leading by example and holding you accountable for goals. If you want your family relationships to improve, then you need to hang around those who reflect what you want your home life to look like. If you want your health to improve, then your best friends had better not be Ronald McDonald and Duncan Hines. *Are you with me?* Ask yourself, who am I around? How are they impacting my life in the areas that I find most important?

> "He who walks with the wise grows wise, but a companion of fools suffers harm."
> Proverbs 13:20

3. What environment am I choosing to live in?

You Are Not A Tree!

Everyone loves a "rags to riches" story — one where all the odds are stacked against a person yet they are somehow able to remove themselves from a bad environment and create the life that they set out to have. It all starts with changing the environment! Sometimes the dream in your heart is bigger than the environment in which you find yourself. Sometimes you have to get out of that environment in order to see your dream fulfilled. The environment must be conducive to the growth that we desire. Just as our muscles grow better in the gym than they do on the couch, and flowers grow better in sunlight than they do in the dark, our success hinges on the environment that we choose to live in.

Joel Osteen said in his book *Become a Better You*, "Consider an oak tree. If you plant it in a pot, its growth will be limited. Once its roots fill that pot, it can grow no further. The problem is not with the tree; it is with the environment."[3] When you need more room to grow, you have to change your environment.

The three most important conditions to keep in mind when you are evaluating whether or not your environment is conducive for growth are:

A vision of what's ahead.

In an environment conducive to growth, we will always be encouraged to look forward to where we are going, not back at where we have been. It is a good idea to build off of yesterday; it is a bad idea to live off of

> In an environment conducive to growth, we will always be encouraged to look forward to where we are going, not back at where we have been.

it. In other words, you can look back to gain some encouragement and confidence from past wins, but just don't stare.

A challenge to grow daily.

My grandparents' house had a real wood fireplace. As a kid I use to love to stir up the fire with what my granddaddy called the poker. You see, a poker is made of iron, not hot at all on its own... it is where you put it that determines its heat. Do you know how to get a poker hot? Put it next to the fire. You know how to keep a poker hot? Keep it next to the fire. You see, we are like the iron in a poker. If our environment is cold, then we will be cold. If our environment is hot, then we will be hot. If our environment is one that is growing, then in turn we will grow. Put yourself in an environment that's hot... where others are ahead of you, where others are growing, where people desire change, and where you are challenged to get out of your comfort zone. It's not always comfortable to associate with people "larger" than we currently are, but it's always profitable. Put yourself where it's *hot*.

A support system.

In an environment conducive to growth, the people around you will be affirming and encouraging. These people will not only model growth for you, they will help nourish and cultivate you to do the same. Planting yourself inside a great support system is like planting your seed of greatness in good soil. This is so important because it doesn't matter how great the potential in the seed, if you don't put it in good soil it will not take root and grow.

4. Am I seeking advice from credible mentors?

Be a Copycat!

In the game of life, people seldom improve when they have no other model but themselves to copy. Being a copycat is great, as long as you are copying the right cat.

To choose great mentors, those who are worthy of emulating, look for those who:

Have mastered the skills you aspire to master.

Have achieved the results you aim to achieve.

Hold themselves to the high standards you hold yourself to.

Like I said before, experience is the best teacher. No longer is this just an old saying for me; I now truly understand it. I understand that I don't have to personally experience everything to LEARN the lesson from it; I can LEARN from others' wins and losses and avoid making poor choices simply by seeking advice from those who've gone before me. This understanding holds true for you as well. I would encourage you to seek advice from credible mentors and LEARN from their experiences as well as your own.

> **Seek advice from credible mentors and LEARN from their experiences as well as your own.**

Model Yourself After The Very Best!

When I played baseball growing up, I always tried to emulate the actions of those who were the very best. From my behavior, how I swung the bat, how I threw the ball, and even my work ethic, I tried to imitate those who had mastered the skills I aspired to master. I did the same thing when I started teaching and coaching. I modeled myself after the teachers and coaches who were habitual winners, those who had achieved the results that I aimed to achieve. It followed suit when I started my network marketing business. I sought to model myself after those who had mastered the skills, achieved the results, and held themselves and the people around them to high standards.

Three Ways To Seek Advice From Mentors:

A. Study what they do.

One of the best ways to get advice, from mentors that you either *do* or *do not* personally know, is to simply study their actions. What did they do to achieve the results? John Maxwell is masterful at duplicating leaders. As a network marketer I am always looking for ways to help build the leadership inside the organization. John created a personal mentoring group called *The Circle*, which I have the privilege to be a part of. I watched how he did it, mixed in my own flavor, and then launched my own mentoring group called *The Nest* in 2013.

B. Listen to what they have to say.

My first six months in network marketing while I was still a full time teacher, I used my planning period to listen to a CD by Jim Rohn, "How to Build your Network Marketing Business." Every day, every week, every month for six months, I listened to his advice. You think that made a difference? You better believe it did. I was receiving great advice from a mentor whom I had never met, and never did get the honor to meet in person. You can do this too, simply by listening to the audios and reading the books that are made available to anyone who

> Take advantage of the resources these mentors are providing; they are giving the advice, but it's up to you to go and listen.

chooses to take advantage. Another great way to listen to the advice of your chosen mentors is by going to their seminars and workshops. Take advantage of the resources these mentors are providing; they are giving the advice, but it's up to you to go and listen.

C. Ask the right questions.

I was able to seek tons of advice about my network marketing business from Paul Orberson simply by asking one simple question: *"What should I expect to happen next?"* Paul has been like a prophet for me in my business. Nearly every time I went to him with questions, he would paint a crystal-clear picture of what I should be prepared for and how I should respond to the situations that I would likely be facing in my near future. Talk about an advantage. What a benefit it is to know what is about to happen and what might be coming next. Now you can prepare.

Guidelines To Follow When Asking Questions Of A Mentor:

- **Always respect his or her time by preparing and delivering the questions you have for them in advance.**

- **When you meet...LISTEN, don't talk. You want their advice; you only get that by allowing them to do the talking.**

During my most recent mentoring session with John Maxwell, I followed the guidelines above. I submitted two pages of questions that I had for him three days before our scheduled meeting. The moment we sat down in the vehicle to leave for dinner and an Atlanta Falcons game, John pulled out a copy of the questions I had emailed to him and said, "Enough small talk, let's get to what you really want to know." He shot pearl after pearl to me from the questions I'd submitted. I never had to say a word; I kept my mouth shut and soaked in every detail he shared. Do you think that backseat session was powerful? You'd better believe it. In a thirty-minute ride to the stadium, because of preparation, intentionality, and listening, John knocked out all of my questions and provided game-changing value and connections that have propelled my forward growth. Once we arrived, we were able to relax and enjoy the game, because business was taken care of.

5. Am I Being a Good Example?

Don't Tell Them, Show Them!

The last question that I ask myself on a regular basis to make sure that I am maintaining consistent growth is, "Am I being a good example?" In other words, am I modeling the expectation for others? In network marketing and in life, we must be willing to be the example. Leading by example, from the front, gives you credibility. You cannot ask people to do what you yourself are not willing to do. Everyone is a leader to some extent, and a rule of thumb for every leader is this:

What your people see is what your people will be.

It is a fact that people will imitate our actions long before they will listen to our words. I spent the summer trying to teach my daughter, Maddie, how to swim. I'd say, "Maddie, one arm then the other. Kick your feet. Now, put your face in the water." She wasn't catching on, and I was getting frustrated. It wasn't until I got in the water, and SHOWED her what I had been TELLING her to do, that she started to make progress. I guess the saying is true, "A pint of example is worth a gallon of advice."

The greatest teacher and leader to have ever walked the earth validates the power of being the example for others to follow. Jesus, time after time, told the people of Israel how to treat one another... but He knew that wasn't enough. Scripture tells us that He went a step further and pointed out to his disciples in John 13:15, "I have set you an example, that you should do as I have done for you."

Abundance Is Available For Anyone!

Like I said earlier, people often assume that abundance is only for the few, the lucky ones, the ones who were born with talents that not everyone has. WRONG! Abundance is available for anyone who is intentional about LEARNING and continual growth. Your success will seldom exceed your personal development. What you become directly influences what you have. Anything of significance is not going to be easy, but we can make it simple by taking on the challenge one bite at a time. So, be intentional about LEARNING and personal growth.

Ask Yourself Regularly:

1. **What am I feeding my mind?**

2. **Who am I hanging around?**

3. **What environment am I choosing to live in?**

4. **Am I seeking advice from credible mentors?**

5. **Am I being a good example for others to model after?**

Learn Points to Remember...

- What am I feeding my mind?

  o Mind meal plan

- Who am I hanging around?

  o Associations

- What environment am I choosing to live in?

  o You are not a tree!

- Am I seeking advice from credible mentors?

  o Be a copycat

- Am I being a good example?

  o Don't tell them, show them

5

a.p.p.l.E.

"E" stands for EVALUATE

"Constant refinement is necessary for continual improvement."
- Chris D. Estes

When I played college baseball, I would occasionally go into what it is called a "slump". Meaning, I couldn't hit the ball even if they put it on a tee for me. When those slumps happened, I would assess my swing to see why it wasn't working. My hopes were always that with just a few slight adjustments I would be back on track. You see, whether in sports, in life, or in business, you must assess if you want to make progress.

In a Slump!

Early in my network marketing business, I was in a slump. I had gone four weeks in a row without anyone wanting to join the business *or* try the products. What I should have done at that point, *which seems obvious now*, was STOP and EVALUATE the issue by asking myself some questions. How many people have I talked to? Am I keeping it simple? Am I performing the *FUNdamental 5*? Am I being consistent? All great questions that would have saved a lot of time, headache, and stress. But I didn't; instead I kept on doing what I had been doing. Have you ever kept doing the same thing expecting a different result? Insanity, right? We've been told *don't quit, keep doing it, keep moving.* Can I give you some advice from personal experience?

If you're moving in the wrong direction,

if you're working and not seeing any results,

if you're swinging and missing, shooting and not scoring...

STOP and EVALUATE.

What's The Score?

You see, everything we do in life from play to work has its own set of rules and its own definition of success. In sports we may measure success in points. In network marketing we may measure success in volume created, our pin rank, or the number of people enrolled as customers or distributors. No matter what the endeavor, there's always a score to measure. We have already covered how to create the best plan to lead you toward success, but your plan just tells you what you want to happen... the "score" tells you what really is happening. The "score" of your game, whatever it may be, is very important. But in order to track the numbers, track the progress, track the results, and know the overall success, we must take time to EVALUATE.

Set aside time to ask yourself these questions:

What am I doing that's working?

What am I doing that's not working?

What can I do to improve?

Take Bite #5

The fifth bite of the A.P.P.L.E. that I eat every day stands for the word EVALUATE. The game of life is always changing. What worked for you yesterday will soon be an outdated strategy. This means that you must make adjustments on a regular basis to improve yourself and your situation. You see, constant refinement is necessary for continual improvement. Never discount the importance of questioning yourself regularly. In this chapter I will walk you through the EVALUATION process I use to make sure I always know the "score" of my game and am always aware of where I can be better. My hope is that you will realize the importance of EVALUATION and allow me to coach you so that you too can recognize your errors and make adjustments.

Constant refinement is necessary for continual improvement.

Take Time to Reflect

Over the past few years I have been very diligent about taking time to reflect on all of the experiences that I've had. I want to EVALUATE the life lessons learned from the good, the bad, and the ugly. I have been very fortunate to have some great mentors who have taken time to share with me their life experiences so that I could learn from their wins and losses as well as my own. I consider the wisdom that they've shared with me a true gift; actually, one of the greatest gifts that you can give to others is the gift of your experiences. The key is that you must remember your experiences in order to pass them on. The best way I have found to remember the lessons of the past, is to take time to reflect and EVALUATE.

Again, if this is your first go-round at life planning, I would encourage you to start small... and then build on the amount of time that you set aside to EVALUATE as you go. The key is that you *start*. Every day, instead of twenty minutes, start with five. Weekly and monthly, instead of a couple of hours, start with thirty minutes. And, quarterly, instead of a long weekend, start with an hour. Then build on these time blocks as your life permits.

Daily Reflection, take 20 minutes...

Finish Strong

At the end of every day I have a routine that I go through that I call my *Finish Strong* routine. First, I take a handful of minutes to review what did and didn't get done that day. Next, I review my schedule for the next day, adding the carryover items that didn't get done today and making any necessary adjustments. Last, I read a few more pages of a good book.

Take What You "Earn"!

This daily reflection is not just abstract thoughts; it's black and white and recorded on my Weekly Activity Tracker... a check mark if I did the activity and a big fat X if I didn't. Remember, this information is for your eyes only... you have to be honest about it and you have to know your true numbers. You decide what works best for you, but this is when I question myself. The following are just a few examples of the questions I use to get myself calibrated. You should develop some that are specific to your goals:

Did I take all five bites out of my A.P.P.L.E. today?

Did I perform the *FUNdamental 5*?

Did I add value to people today?

Check it off, and then see how those numbers compare to what you said you needed to do each day on your Life Plan in order to reach your goals by the deadlines that you set.

WEEKLY ACTIVITY TRACKER

Activity	M	T	W	TH	F	ST	SN
FAITH							
READ BIBLE	✓	✗	✓	✓			
FINANCE							
TOUCH 5	✓	✓	✗	✓			
PROSPECT 3	✗	✓	✓	✗			

Let me tell you something exciting: if you know your numbers... if you know your "score" for today, you can be better tomorrow.

Weekly and Monthly Reflection, take a couple hours...

Sunday Prep

At the end of every week, which is on Sunday for me, I take a couple of hours to EVALUATE my activities from the previous week and map out my calendar for the upcoming week. I like to call this *Sunday Prep*. This is a time to reflect back AND look ahead.

Reflect Back...

First, I reflect back by tallying the numbers from the previous week so that I know the "score" of my game. I must reiterate, this is a black and white process. I just want the facts, and they are found in the numbers. Remember, your planned activities for the week should correlate to the goals you set on your Life Plan in each of the Buckets you identified. If not, something is off. This is where most people who have joined the 3% get into trouble. *Let me remind you that only 3% of people even write down their goals and begin the process of planning their life; the other 97% are just wandering aimlessly, waiting to see what happens.* But many of the 3% who do write their goals down quickly fall off course because their daily and weekly activities don't relate to their goals and their plan. That's why it's so important each day to eat your A.P.P.L.E. with a final focus on EVALUATE.

Look Ahead...

Next, I look ahead. I use the time during *Sunday Prep* to fill out the preparation tools for the upcoming week (Weekly Activity Tracker, Weekly To Do list, and Daily Time Budgets). With these tools in hand at the start of each new week, I can more easily stay on course and headed toward the goals I have set for myself. As I'm filling out my tools for the upcoming week, I am once again questioning myself:

How many days this past week did I take all five bites out of my A.P.P.L.E.?

How can I be better this upcoming week?

Where do I need to be intentional about making improvements?

Just so you know, I have yet to have a week where *everything* that I put on my Daily Time Budgets and my

Weekly To Do List gets accomplished. I always have an item or two that either gets carried over to the next week, delegated out to someone else, or trashed because its time has passed.

Make Note Of Your Weakest Areas.

During *Sunday Prep,* I also make sure to note any key area for improvement. For example, if I earned an X (or two) the previous week because I didn't talk to the people on the days I was supposed to with my *Touch 5* program, I know that this upcoming week, doing so needs to be a key area of focus. It's much easier to course-correct when you are just slightly off track than when you're ten tracks over. Believe me, I know what it's like to be ten tracks over in multiple Buckets... it's not fun.

Quarterly and Yearly Reflection, take a long weekend...

Calibration Vacation

At the end of every quarter, I take a long weekend — three or four days — and go on what I call a Calibration Vacation, to get a handle on the direction my life is headed in all areas. I find that it is important to have time once every three months away from all distractions to really get clarity on what adjustments or corrections need to be made to keep me moving toward my visions, hopes, and dreams. In other words, a Calibration Vacation is a time to reflect, refuel, and regain control.

Reflect, Refuel, And Regain Control!

Taking Time Away Allows You To:

Reflect:

Paul Orberson often said, "Now, Chris, it's ok to look back; just don't stare." While you are away, take time to reflect back on the accomplishments of the quarter. Be happy about the progress you are making and celebrate your wins... but just for a moment.

Refuel:

When your vehicle runs low on fuel, you don't fill it up while driving down the highway. You have to *stop* at a service station to refuel. The same applies to your life; in order to refuel your creative mind you must *stop* (step away from the hustle and bustle of the everyday) and just *think*. One of my favorite parts about Calibration Vacation is the time I set aside to add fresh new ideas to the projects I already have going on. My favorite "gas station" is the lazy river. Some of my best ideas have been formed with my backside parked in an inner tube, eyes closed, toes in the water, floating around with the sun on my face. You have to discover your own lazy river, whatever place it is that you can relax and just *think*. You see, most people are always so busy (notice I said busy, not productive) that there is never time for them to think, to come up with new ideas, or to see new opportunities that are right in front of them. Heck, I was like that for a while. Don't let that be you. Take time to refuel your creative mind and spark new ideas with some intentional *thinking* time.

> **Take time to refuel your creative mind and spark new ideas with some intentional *thinking* time.**

Regain control:

Calibration Vacation is also an essential component of time management. Remember, as discussed in the earlier chapter on preparation, you must manage *yourself* first. When life's demands start to push you off path or tempt you to invest time in non-essential tasks... step back and regain control by getting re-calibrated. I don't just float the lazy river for three to four full days; I also have intentional time set aside to really reflect back on the last three months. I go prepared to analyze that quarter's Weekly Activity Trackers and Daily Time Budgets. Once I have gone through all of the numbers, I do a time audit (which we will discuss in just a second) and compare the findings to what I did the previous quarter.

Hitting the mark with 100% accuracy is not the only way to have a successful quarter; success for me is progress. Was I better this quarter than I was last quarter? What areas still need improving? Did my daily activities correlate to my goals on my Life Plan? I write down any adjustments that need to be made on what I call a Course Corrector. This sheet I review, along with my Life Plan and other tools each morning, as a reminder of where I need to be better in order to maintain forward movement.

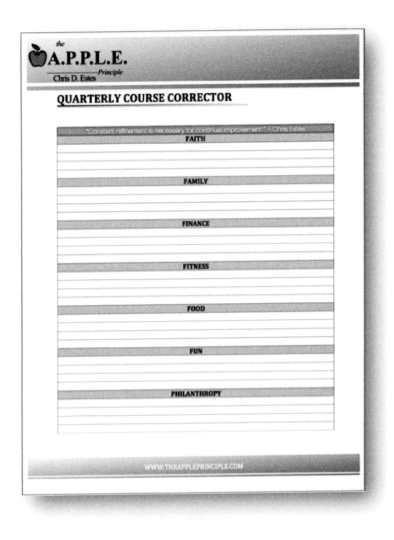

Get Calibrated!

The primary purpose of a Calibration Vacation isn't to play or simply find bliss, *although those are happy side effects*. The purpose is to reflect, refuel, and regain control. Just try it. I promise you'll be amazed at how much more motivated, productive, and fulfilled you will be by scheduling time every quarter to get calibrated. You may be thinking to yourself, "I

124

can't take four days every quarter and go off just to get calibrated." I totally understand that. You don't have start with four days; you can start with just one day locked in your house without distractions. Heck, start with a couple hours. The point is to get yourself some isolation. For now, start with what you *can* do... then work yourself up to longer periods of time further away from the distractions of the everyday.

Time Audit

Over the past few years I have come to truly understand the value of an hour of my time. This understanding led me to take inventory of where my time was allocated so that I could keep doing the main things, delegate some tasks that were important but not in my strength zone, and finally remove altogether some things that were truly time wasters.

One item that I used to invest several hours a week in was typing up notes from books that I had read and personal development audios that I had listened to. These notes are very important to me because they play a role in the creation of my trainings and aid in my own personal development. During my time audit, it was unveiled to me, however, that the actual task of typing them is something that could be delegated out. I reached out to several people and found someone who would be willing, for an hourly fee, to type these notes for me. In the end, I still have my notes. And more importantly, I have gained time back that can now be used for the big rocks in my life and business.

Take time out each quarter to audit how you are using your time. Are you investing time in activities that are important but others could do for you? Are you wasting time on things that don't move you any closer to your ultimate goals? Take control by taking action on the *MUST DO's* and *SHOULD DO's*, delegating the *COULD DO's*, and ditching the rest.

Like I said before, constant refinement is necessary for continual improvement. In order to know where refinement is needed, we must inspect what we expect. Go over your actions with a fine-toothed comb knowing that high intention deserves high attention.

How often are you actually taking all five bites out of your A.P.P.L.E.? After all, to keep the doctor away, you can't just eat half of an apple every day, or a whole apple every third day. It's a guarantee that your plan won't work if you don't work it. Learn from my mistakes here. Too many times I let days, weeks, and months pass, traveling down the wrong road because I was too "busy" to stop and EVALUATE. Begin developing the habit of eating your A.P.P.L.E. every day, with a final focus on EVALUATE. Remember, a small bite is better than no bite. Get started and get excited because your daily, weekly, monthly, and quarterly course corrections will help you stay on the path to your version of success in life and in business.

Evaluate Points to Remember...

- Daily reflection, take 20 minutes...
  - o Finish Strong
- Weekly and monthly reflection, take a couple hours...
  - o Sunday Prep
- Quarterly and yearly reflection, take a long weekend...
  - o Calibration Vacation
  - o Quarterly Course Corrector

Conclusion

Back in 2008, when I was broke, working a full-time job building someone else's dreams, and raising everyone else's kids...

If someone would have told me that by the end of 2013 I would...

Be retired from traditional employment for good.

Be making millions of dollars residually each year.

Have the freedom, choices, and options to do what I want, when I want, where I want, with whom I want, as often as I want.

Be personal friends with the likes of John Maxwell and Paul Orberson.

Be personally mentoring top network marketing leaders.

Speak and train on stage in front of thousands of people on a regular basis.

Be a published author.

... I would have laughed in their face!

But guess what? All of that has happened for me in the past five years. Now, anytime I'm asked questions like:

How are you?

What have you been up to?

What's new?

My reply is always, "You wouldn't believe me if I told you!" I say that, not to impress you, but to impress upon you the fact that your next five years can be totally different than your last five, if you choose for them to be.

I still pinch myself some days to make sure I'm not daydreaming. Now don't be mistaken, my success didn't happen overnight, it didn't happen without great intentionality and consistency, it didn't come without a steep price, and it didn't come easy... but it was definitely worth it.

Is there anything special about me? NO. Have I achieved any accomplishment that is out of reach for anyone reading this book? Absolutely NOT. In fact, I'm just an ordinary person who was able to achieve some extraordinary things by leveraging the power of *The A.P.P.L.E. Principle.*

Rewrite the future for yourself and your loved ones by choosing to take all five bites out of your A.P.P.L.E. everyday:

Bite #1:

Choose to have a winning ATTITUDE no matter the circumstance. Plant seeds of increase into your life and the lives of those around you on a daily basis. Recite your personal commercial and douse yourself in confidence every morning.

Bite #2:

PREPARE your days for success. Define what success really means for you in all the Buckets of your life. Work backward from your long-range goals until you know the actions you need to take each day to progress you on your path toward success. Allocate your time each day to the things that matter most, the things that you *Must Do* in order to have success.

Bite #3:

PERFORM the actions everyday. Follow your plan even when you don't feel like it.

Bite #4:

LEARN something new everyday to insure you are growing better and bigger. Ask yourself these five questions below:

1. What am I feeding my mind?

2. Who am I hanging around?

3. What environment am I choosing to live in?

4. Am I seeking advice from credible mentors?

5. Am I being a good example for others to model themselves after?

Bite #5:

EVALUATE your progress and actions; determine where you could be better. Take time to reflect on the actions you are taking. Are they producing results? Are they moving you forward? If not, STOP and make some course corrections sooner rather than later.

I want to encourage you to start NOW and eat your A.P.P.L.E. today. Then be consistent and intentional with your actions every day moving forward. And if you do this, it's my belief that your best days are just ahead...

so get your HOPES up!

The A.P.P.L.E. Principle

Resources

Introduction

1. Ziglar, Zig. *Zig On...This Way To Greatness.* Ziglar Newsletter, Edition 28. 21 Jul. 2009.

Attitude

1. Maxwell, John C. *The Difference Maker: Making Your Attitude Your Greatest Asset* (Nashville: Thomas Nelson, 2006).

2. Osteen, Joel. *Become A Better You: 7 Keys To Improving Your Life Every Day* (Philadelphia: Running Press Book Publishers, 2010).

3. Lover, Samuel, and James, Jeffrey Roche. *The Collected Works of Samuel Lover* (Pennsylvania: Little, Brown, 1903), 188.

4. Acuff, John. *Start: Punch Fear in the Face, Escape Average, and Do Work That Matters* (Nashville: Thomas Nelson, 2013).

5. Maraboli, Steve. "Motivational." SteveMaraboli.com. A Better Today, Inc, 2012.

6. *Rocky V.* Dir. John G. Alvildsen. Perf. Sylvester Stallone, Talia Shire, and Burt Young. Star Partners III, Ltd/MGM/UA Distribution Company, VHS. 1990.

7. Swindoll, Charles. *Day By Day* (Nashville: Thomas Nelson, 2005), 17.

8. Osteen, Joel. *Become A Better You: 7 Keys To Improving Your Life Every Day* (Philadelphia: Running Press Book Publishers, 2010).

9. Achor, Shawn. *The Happiness Advantage: The Seven Principles of Positive Psychology That Fuel Success and Performance at Work* (New York: Crown Business, 2010).

10. Ziglar, Zig. *See You At The Top* (Louisiana: Pelican, 2000).

Prepare

1. Olson, Jeff. *The Slight Edge: Secret to a Successful Life* (Ohio: Momentum Media, 2005).

2. Ziglar, Zig. *See You At The Top* (Louisiana: Pelican, 2000), 317.

3. Canfield, Jack, and Switzer, Janet. *The Success Principles: How to Get from Where You Are to Where You Want to Be* (New York: Harper Collins, 2009).

4. Berger, Rick. *OK, You Dummies, Up Against The Wall!* (Bloomington: Xlibris Corporation, 2008).

Perform

1. Canfield, Jack, and Switzer, Janet. *The Success Principles: How to Get from Where You Are to Where You Want to Be* (New York: Harper Collins, 2009).

2. Klemmer, Brian. *The Compassionate Samurai: Being Extraordinary in an Ordinary World* (Carlsbad: Hay House, 2009).

3. Maxwell, John C. *Winning With People: Discover the People Principles that Work for You Every Time* (Nashville, Thomas Nelson, 2005).

Learn

1. Maxwell, John C. *The 15 Invaluable Laws of Growth: Live Them and Reach Your Potential.* (Nashville: Center Street, 2012).

2. Schwartz, David. *The Magic Of Thinking Big.* (New York: Simon and Schuster, 1987).

3. Osteen, Joel. *Become A Better You: 7 Keys To Improving Your Life Every Day.* (Philadelphia: Running Press, 2010).

The A.P.P.L.E. Principle

About the Author

Chris D. Estes is a multimillion-dollar earner in the profession of Network Marketing. With no prior network marketing experience, he built an organization exceeding 100,000 team members and customers in less than five years. Chris is the founder of Team Elite (www.TeamElite.net), a team inside the network marketing company he represents. Chris serves on the Distributor Leadership Council and has been awarded "Distributor of the Year" honors twice in his company.

Chris graduated from Lindsey Wilson College in Columbia, Kentucky where he presently serves on the board of trustees. In 2013 he started *The Nest*, his personal mentoring group, as a platform to teach and hold accountable those who qualify, on the principle taught in this book.

Currently, Chris travels the world speaking, training, and mentoring. He is a dynamic leader who lives out the motto, "Service to many leads to greatness!"

He can be followed here:
www.twitter.com/chrisestes_1
www.facebook.com/chris.estes
www.ChrisDEstes.com
www.TheApplePrinciple.com